PRAISE FOR
YOUR DAILY LIFE IS YOUR TEMPLE

Anne Rowthorn takes us on a journey in which she generously shares stories of her own passionate involvement with the everyday wonders and tragedies of life in God's world, and by the end of it we realize she has given us the gift of eyes better able to perceive footprints of the Holy in our own lives.

> PAUL MINUS, President, Coalition for Ministry
> in Daily Life and author of *Taking Faith To Work*

Your Daily Life is Your Temple will break you out of the spiritual box and challenge your notions of what spirituality is, where you find it, and how you practice it.

> GREGORY F. AUGUSTINE PIERCE,
> President and Co-Publisher of ACTA Publications and
> author of *Finding God@Work* and *Spirituality@Work*

Rowthorn shows that our spirituality is not individually constructed from within, but derived from our family, community, and work milieu—from the fabric of ordinary life.

> WILLIAM DROEL, founder of National Center for the Laity
> in Chicago and author of *Full-Time Christians:*
> *The Real Challenge From Vatican II*

Rowthorn integrates the wisdom of many faiths and cultures through stories about family, work, friends, children, money, environment, justice, and hospitality. It's like a walk with a friend in the woods on a sunny day.

> SALLY SIMMEL, Evangelical Lutheran Church
> in America, consultant, and workshop leader

Anne Rowthorn throws open the doors and windows of our limited, institutional understandings of the spiritual life and lets fresh breezes blow through the temples of our daily lives. *Your Daily Life is Your Temple* is refreshing, challenging, and liberating.

> CAROLINE A. WESTERHOFF, author of *Make All Things New,*
> *Calling: A Song for the Baptized,* and *Good Fences*

In this book of reflections on a lived faith, you will discover an enduring spirituality of everyday life that "builds up the commonwealth of God." An important and fine book.

> JAMES A. KOWALSKI, Dean, Cathedral of St. John the Divine

A gifted storyteller, with a sharp e~~ ~~~~ ~~~~ ~~ ~~~~ ~~ ~~
in everyday life. From remote villages i~
the street, Rowthorn has learned to l~
her midst.

> DOUGL
> E:

D1261058

Lesley +

Your Daily Life is Your Temple

"Your daily life is your religion and your temple."
—Kahlil Gibran

Your Daily Life
is Your Temple

Anne Rowthorn

SEABURY BOOKS
an imprint of Church Publishing, Inc., New York

Library of Congress Cataloging-in-Publication Data

Rowthorn, Anne W.
Your daily life is your temple / Anne Rowthorn.
    p.   cm.
Includes bibliographical references.
ISBN 1-59627-022-5
1. Christian life. I. Title.
BV4501.3.R69 2006
248.4--dc22

                        2006006022

Church Publishing Incorporated
445 Fifth Avenue
New York, New York 10016
www.churchpublishing.org

To
Anna,
Jackson,
Nathaniel,
Beckett,
and
Juliette,
with dearest love.

Table of Contents

Acknowledgments

It takes a community to write a book of this sort and I am grateful beyond measure to my community of friends, family, colleagues, and acquaintances. They have generously shared their stories, their experiences, and their insights with me. My life and this book are all the richer because of their generosity in sharing of themselves.

The book got its initial boost from my time as a Visiting Fellow at the Episcopal Theological Seminary of the Southwest. Special thanks are owed to the Very Rev. Titus Presler, who was the dean at the time, as well as to Rob Cogswell, seminary librarian, and to my mentor and good friend, Russell Schulz.

I am indebted to Bob Graham, United States Senator from Florida, who illustrated for me the significance of daily work which laid the foundation for my theology of work. Students in my various classes at the Hartford Seminary provided examples of how faith is lived in the workplace, especially Dave Koppel, Geordie Campbell, Warren Bouton, Martin Montonye, and Greg Wismar. And there were others I interviewed when I worked as a writer for the Episcopal Church USA's Mission Discernment Project, especially Ed Todd, a commercial fisherman, Jessica Wilson, a librarian, and Marion Ridley, a surgeon.

Christopher Allen-Doucet and his twelve-year-old son, Micah, provided a courageous and compassionate example from their own lives of how, in Chris's words, "It's not enough to know there's suffering in the world. We need to be agents for change to end that suffering." Rosemary Feerick of Harvest Time, Davis L. Fisher of MoneyTree Consulting, and Joy Linscheid of Funding Exchange provided essential resources for the chapter on money. Courtney Bourns helped with both that chapter and the one on friendship. I am grateful to the Honorable Byron Rushing of the Massachusetts House of Representatives for his insights into the life and passions of a working politician. The members of my Lambeth Conference small group taught me about the lengths to which individuals will go to forgive their enemies, and I especially thank Dr. Grace Mukamwezi of Kigali, Rwanda.

Artists have opened my doors to perception by illustrating how the arts lead people to the heart of God. Especially I thank my friends, poet Elizabeth Allan and artist Asa Oddsdóttir. I thank my neighbors in Paris who reached over the barriers of language and culture to become my friends: Raymonde Vautrin, Madeleine La Fol, Janine and Jacques Pélissier, and my café friend, Nanette. I thank other friends, especially Judy and Walter Conley, Clare Davis, Bob and Mary Baker and Beatrice Dodge. The central story for the chapter on friends was drawn from a group of friends who were high school students and neighbors in Hamden, Connecticut. I especially thank Patrick Plunkett, John Nutcher, John Hearne, and Michael McCormack, who shared with me the significance of their long and close friendship. Thanks are due also to Gregory F. Augustine Pierce, the author of Spirituality@Work, for the fine account in chapter twelve of the Buddhist woman who became enlightened.

Family members have provided both inspiration and examples used throughout the book: Virginia Rowthorn and her husband, Michael Apel, and their children, Anna and Nathaniel; Christian Rowthorn; and Perry and Hayley Zinn-Rowthorn and their sons, Jackson and Beckett. This book is dedicated to the little ones of the family and to the newest member, Juliette, who as I write is now one week old. They add joy and laughter and lots of fun to my life. The greatest thanks is reserved for my husband, Jeffery Rowthorn, who shared many of the experiences recounted in the book and stood by me as I wrote it. My long marriage to him has been my life's richest blessing.

The book has come to fruition through the friendship and diligence of my indefatigable editor, Cynthia Shattuck. Through sharing hiking trails and a sunny afternoon on a Rhode Island beach, through innumerable e-mails and phone conversations, Cynthia has been there for me and her ideas and suggestions have helped shape the book.

The passionate engagement of all these friends, colleagues, and family has inspired my own passionate engagement in the joyous adventure of living. I treasure them all and I thank them.

Prologue

By spirituality, we mean the way of thinking, living and
sanctifying the acts of our lives.
—Carlo Carretto, *Letters from the Desert*

When I moved to Paris, Madeleine was one of the first people in our new neighborhood to befriend me. She is the glue
who holds it together. She knows all the people who live in
the rabbit warren of little streets and pedestrian walkways,
talks to them, gives them clothes, and worries about them
when they're not doing well. When a neighbor is sick she
brings food. When one is lonely she offers companionship.
She welcomed me and became my friend in our early days in
the city when it was a struggle for me to say anything coher-
ent in French. When my husband and I returned home from
a weekend, we invariably would find a bag hanging on our
doorknob. It contained wonderful fresh farm eggs and leeks,
spinach, juicy tomatoes, fresh garlic, watercress, and oversized
zucchini from her son André's garden in the country.
Madeleine is also a savage critic of any injustice—she has zero
tolerance for pretension or what she calls *snobisme*—and she
never goes to church. Madeleine and so many others like her
on both sides of the Atlantic are spiritual, deeply religious
people who live out their faith in action, but the church does
not figure anywhere in their lives.

I have many friends like Madeleine. They have lost patience with churches whose preachers bore them with irrelevant, poorly prepared sermons that have little bearing on their day-to-day lives, and where any sense of community has long since departed. Yet the people are out there hungering for food that nourishes the soul and thirsting for a religion or philosophy that will offer meaning for their lives. They want to make the connections between their faith in God and every aspect of their existence. They see the quality of life on this planet declining; they see corruption at the top of corporate and political empires; they see their children wandering without direction or hope in the future. So they search for spiritualities that will assuage their anxieties and fuel their quests. People are starving for authentic spiritual food that feeds the soul and deeply nourishes the spirit, food enough for all our brothers and sisters on this planet in all its tastes and colors and multiplicity.

We seek to find where the spirit of God is lively right now, giving life and creating life, and we are ready to join the action. We seek to make common cause with other searchers to find the holy in our midst and to dare a better world, more reflective of what surely the Holy God of the universe intends for all God's beloved creatures. To seek and find God in a myriad of ways every day of our lives, we do not need the labyrinth at Chartres Cathedral. We do not need the vision quest in New Mexico to experience and follow God in our lives. We are more likely to feel our loving God reaching out to us in an encouraging smile of a loved one, in the hug of a child returning home, in the kindness shown us by a complete stranger, in a red sunset lighting up the western sky, and in the still of the descending night. Artists show us how to penetrate reality and open doors to perception, while poets tell us the truth about ourselves and our world. Compassionate workers and ethical politicians, caretakers of children, our friends and those who live God's hospitality of hearth and home and heart all remind us that we seek God who is present among us in our neighbors and in our efforts to build up our communities. Living a spirituality of everyday life in today's world means being anchored in the religion of our tradition whatever that may be, yet also seeking strength and insights from religions very different from our own. It means living life intensely, passionately, with our eyes wide open to the pain and division in our world—yet hopefully, joyfully, and lovingly.

Unlike Madeleine and many of my friends, I still go to church as a seeker and searcher. I also believe that church—or synagogue or temple—is just one source among many for the formation of a vibrant faith, and that it is primarily in the context of our daily lives that we find the rich life of the spirit.

This book is for people like Madeleine who are not church or synagogue goers yet who feel that they are walking a path of faith. It is for also for those of you who still participate in your communities of faith but want more food for the spirit than you are getting on a Sunday morning. It is for anyone who seeks to live passionately and can be coaxed into looking at the ordinary circumstances of your daily routine as building blocks for a more passionate life. Dorothee Soelle, a German theologian, wrote, "There are human beings who not only hear the 'silent cry' which is God, but also make it heard as the music of the world that even to this day fills the cosmos and the soul."[1]

A spirituality of everyday life is everything we do, all day long, that builds up the commonwealth of God. Your daily life is your temple. Together let us open its doors and uncover an authentic spirituality that recognizes all of life as holy. It is already there, just waiting for us to behold and to grasp.

1

A Place Called Home

The mosques and churches float through our memories,
Prayers devoid of sense or taste echo from the walls.
Never has the heart of God been touched by them,
But still beats on amidst the sounds of drums and bells.

Migjenji (Millosh Gjergj Nickolla), an Albanian poet

Benoît was the only child of the owners of our vacation house in Larcat, a remote French village high in the Pyrenees. He was eighteen years old and had just finished his term at the *lycée*. He was returning from a party with his friends and the car missed the turn and tore into a tree. Benoit was the only passenger killed. His parents, whose permanent home was in the city, chose for his funeral the little hillside church in their ancestral village. The villagers, mostly retired folk with deep roots in the hamlet, had all welcomed my husband and me when we first arrived—they invited us to their homes, told us when the baker made his deliveries, brought their spare garden produce by, and warned us that when we heard an almighty roar echoing through the village on a Wednesday morning not to worry, it was only the shrill horn of the butcher making his rounds. Daily they stopped by and gave us progress reports as to how the family was coping with their loss and how the villagers were planning a funeral reception. While we were merely vacationers, they readily incorporated us into their lives, and they assumed we would attend the funeral, just like everyone else.

On the appointed day when the church bells rang out over the hills, my husband and I walked through a desolate group of young people gathered in the churchyard, Benoît's friends, into the church where the elderly villagers were already seated. Several grandmothers with gnarled hands were threading rosary beads between their fingers. At the last minute the young people entered and the service began. Then it struck us forcibly that the only people saying the responses were the elderly—and the two of us! As the priest began the Lord's Prayer, it was the same. Benoît's friends uttered not a word. They were not disrespectful; they did not have an "attitude." They just stood there, immobile and with such sadness in their eyes. They had lost their friend in a terrible accident and they were still in shock. Then the realization hit me: they did not know the Lord's Prayer. They had never been taught it. These were very typical urban French teenagers, well educated and responsible. But their parents had not taken them to church when they were children and for some, this was the first time they had walked through the doors of a church.

At their best, churches present Jesus Christ so compellingly to children that they will experience Christ as a living, active presence in their lives. This did not happen for me, and my guess is that for many people it was the same. But conversion does not matter at this point in a child's life. What does matter is that children be raised in their particular tradition, whatever that may be, and that they absorb its teachings. All those years of catechism, First Communion classes, Sunday school, junior choir, Young People's Fellowship, Christmas pageants, high holy days, and listening to scripture Sunday after Sunday may roll off their backs, little noticed, recognized, or appreciated. But if the tradition in which children grow up does nothing else, it lays a foundation and gives them a treasury of resources to draw on for the rest of their lives.

I think many of us are like the writer Richard Bernstein, the *New York Times* book editor and former *Time* magazine bureau chief in Beijing, who retraced the path of the seventh-century Chinese Buddhist monk Hsuan Tsang. Hsuan went on a pilgrimage to discover the roots of Buddhism in India, where in the sixth century Prince Siddhartha left his noble family and their riches to receive enlightenment in the wilderness. He became the first Buddha: the one who is awake, who is enlightened. Bernstein was captivated by the monk whose only goal was to discover the Ultimate Truth, and what the writer reveals about himself is what probably many of us would say if we were completely honest. Bernstein is obviously a seeker. "In matters of the spirit," he writes, "I am a Jew. I come to all religions as a skeptic, essentially a nonbeliever.... I am a strangely religious nonbeliever, a devout sort of atheist." In spite of this, Bernstein has a religious place he can call home, for he is grounded in the culture of his faith that has stayed with him:

> I am tied to Judaism by *aesthetic sentiment,* by respect for the martyrdom of others, and by a sense of history.... In the antiquity of Judaism, and in the duration of the Jewish conscience, I feel linked in a very long chain, one that stretches way back to the beginning of recorded time. In there is my religious meaning.... After all of the centuries and all of the blood, I do not want it to end here, with me.[2]

Bernstein reminds me of my friend Sarah, who has a large family that gathers from Florida, New York, and New Jersey to celebrate the Seder at her home in Connecticut. This is a high point in the year, and everyone looks forward to it. Yet Sarah told me she does not know whether or not she believes in God and that no member of the family goes to synagogue. So I asked her why, then, does she take such pleasure in the Seder? "Anne, you've got to understand that it's an *identity thing. It's about family.*" Now that I get it, I feel a little envious of my Jewish friends every year when Passover rolls around. I recall a statistics class in which the professor asked the forty or so of us whether we would be at home the next week observing the Seder. Virtually every hand shot up. It felt as if all the world was Jewish, except for me. My guess is that most of my companion students were something like Sarah, observing the Seder and their identity as Jews whether or not they have a well-articulated belief in God. Nonetheless, I am envious. Christians simply have no comparable rite that brings together, around the dining room table, family, fun, distinctive foods and drink, ritual, and the retelling of the ancient stories of the people—all in a rite in which children have distinct roles.

At Passover, every home where the Seder is observed becomes a sanctuary and every common dining table an altar where the history of the liberation of the Jews is told through scripture, literature, legend, folklore, and song. The night of the Seder is different from all other nights. On an ordinary night, the small children eat their dinner, do their homework, and go to bed; on the night of the Seder, they follow their father around the house, removing by candlelight any crumbs of leavened bread. On an ordinary night, they turn off their lights and retire to their dream world; on the night of the Seder, candles light the darkness and they take their part at the table with their elders.

Toward the beginning of the rite, the youngest child who can read asks the traditional four questions—*Why is this night different from all other nights?*—and after three of the four ritual glasses of wine, the bitter herbs, the traditional foods, it is a child again who opens the door to the prophet Elijah, the honored guest at every Seder. In Jewish lore, Elijah never died but was magically carried off to heaven. He is said to be the champion of the oppressed; he brings hope, cheer, and relief to the needy, and he performs miracles of rescue and deliverance. After the door is closed and the fourth glass of wine is poured, children who are very observant will notice that there is a little less wine in the cup reserved for Elijah, a sure indication that he is with them at this Seder.

My own family has two customs that are our household identity rites. One is the table blessing over the evening meal, and the other is our Thanksgiving Day thanksgivings. When the children were young, Jeffery and I wanted a table blessing that would be simple for them to learn and remember. With the dinner ready, we would pause, hold hands around the table, and say, "God is great; God is good; and we thank him for our food." And we would add, "and God bless Granny and Uncle Jay," naming grandparents and family members who were absent from the table, and ending with "and all of us."

This worked well for years and years, and the families of any guests who were dining with us were incorporated into the grace. But when the children were in junior high school we decided to write a new grace that was less simple and childlike, that was better liturgy, and that would make our Jewish friends feel welcome. Their reaction was immediate and decisive: they weren't having it! How could we take away the grace that had become such a familiar family practice? Why didn't we ask them? The new grace was summarily discarded. In retrospect, our mistake was that Jeffery and I had underestimated, in Sarah's words, "the identity thing." Our simple little prayer had become part of the children's *passive vocabulary of faith;* it was their place called home. Now they are in their late thirties and some of them have children of their own, but the table ritual never changes. When they are home these hulking six-feet-four-inch men and their sophisticated sister, along with their partners and children and friends, will sit down to the Rowthorn dining table, clasp hands, and say, "God is great; God is good; . . ." When we get to the final phrase asking for a blessing on "all of us" the little ones will smile at each other and give their hands an extra shake. If there is any lesson to be learned it is this: if you want good liturgy, do it right from the beginning!

A family ritual that we feel a little more proud of is our Thanksgiving Day thanksgivings. The board has been laid with food and floral offerings of friends and family. A large turkey adorns the center, dressed up with its cranberry necklace and surrounded by the usual traditional side dishes—the creamed onions, mashed potatoes, wild rice, yams, nuts, and

e household now gathers around the table. We
everyone who wishes, including the children, offers
prayer or phrase in thanksgiving for the blessings they
have received since the last Thanksgiving Day. Life's changes
and achievements and pleasures are offered up, along with
prayers for family members and friends. The little ones thank
God for new puppies and babies on the way, their elders
remember family members who have passed on. At the conclusion, one member reads the closing collect, which begins,
"Blessed are you, O Holy God of the Universe. You in your
goodness sustain the whole world with grace, loving-kindness,
and compassion. We thank you that you have sustained us and
all our loved ones since last Thanksgiving Day. . . ." There have
been times when Jeffery and I have wondered how this ritual
was sitting with the children, and there were a few times when
they would mutter, "Oh, do we have to do this *again?*"
However, a couple of years ago Chris was living in Kyoto and
celebrated Thanksgiving with a group of his American and
Japanese friends. All was set out to behold and just as the company was about to dive in, Chris suggested they hold hands
around the table and recite their Thanksgiving Day thanksgivings. It was a place called home, far away from home.

The traditions we experience as children with our families
remain with us the rest of our lives. My memories are filled
with the sights and sounds and smells of my childhood
church: the habits, the teachings, the music, the chanting, the
silence, the aroma of incense, the light of burning votive candles. Ornate statues of the Virgin, melodies of psalms that
echo in my head, fragments of scripture that steal into consciousness throughout the day and comfort me during a
sleepless night. Remembrances of weddings and baptisms,
funerals, the bareness of Good Fridays and glorious Easters,
every corner of the church flowered and fragrant, and my
First Communion on my ninth birthday. All these activities,
memories, and teachings, absorbed over a lifetime, have
planted a bountiful garden within, and I draw on its fruits
every day of my life—and in particular during times of crisis.

On an ordinary Sunday when I was about eleven years old, the priest visited my Sunday school class and handed out to the children copies of the Prayer of St. Francis of Assisi. He told us to memorize it, and there it stays, embedded in my memory. Perhaps more than any other prayer, psalm, or scriptural phrase, this prayer—"Lord, make us instruments of your peace…"—has shaped my conscience and guided my actions throughout my whole life. Such is the passive vocabulary of my religious life, and if you grew up in an observant family of any tradition, you will have your own. The totality of our religious tradition creates what Bernstein calls "aesthetic sentiment." It is there to nurture us throughout our lives. My concern for the young friends of Benoît is that they never developed the passive vocabulary of their faith, so when tragedy strikes they are left empty-handed.

■   ▒   ▒

Almost everyone has a place they can call home, a spiritual home. If I could take myself back to Benoît's funeral and the gathering of his friends, I would ask them about their family customs. If they still had grandmothers or great-grandmothers living, I would suggest that they talk with them and ask them about the spiritual traditions of their families. While their parents may not have passed on a spiritual heritage, almost every family has spiritual roots of some sort, though for some it takes more sleuthing to find them. If there is truly nothing there in the family, then we need to look elsewhere because everyone needs a place called home. Otherwise we spend our lives living on the shores of others' experiences, never grounded, never secure. If Benoît's friends could not find spiritual traditions within their families, then I would ask them if there were any people whom they admired, or if they knew anyone they might consider to be wise—a teacher perhaps, a class advisor, the kindly neighbor who always greets them when they return home from afar, the parent of a friend, the old man tending the community garden, the lady down the street who radiates such warmth. It is never too late to find our way home, or indeed to find a new one.

Whoever we are and wherever we are, everyone needs a place called home; however observant or non-observant we are, we need that anchor. It might be the passive vocabulary of faith such as the simple "God is great; God is good" embedded in the family's collective memory, or the yearly Passover Seder. Or it might mean adopting a new spiritual home, as I would have urged Benoît's friends to do. Our mosques and churches and temples and home rituals float through our memories where the heart of God still beats on amidst the sounds and bells. The first building block of a vibrant spirituality for our time is the place each of us calls home. However far away from home we may wander, either literally or metaphorically, we still call out to God. And deep within our hearts, in our own familiar language, God answers, "I am here. I am with you. Wherever you go, I will go. While you may flee from me, I will always be by your side, loving you, protecting you, encouraging you to taste of the richness of my creation." Grounded in the aesthetic sentiment of our religious roots, we are free to taste the wisdom and delights of others and to look at all of life's circumstances as roads to spiritual enlightenment, opportunities for passionate engagement in every aspect of our lives.

2
Following the Temple Path

*I maintain that every major religion of the world—
Buddhism, Christianity, Confucianism, Hinduism,
Islam, Jainism, Sikhism, Taoism, Zoroastrianism—has
similar ideals of love, the same goal of benefiting
humanity through spiritual practice, and the same
effect of making their followers into better human
beings.*

—Tenzin Gyatso,
the fourteenth Dalai Lama of Tibet

Paradoxically, once we have our place we call home, with
roots in our own faith, we are free to draw on the riches of
other traditions. Anchored in our own religious tradition,
whatever it may be, we can wander Ulysses-like through
other great religions and cultures, seeking inspiration and
understanding. A spirituality for our day thrives in diversity. I
came late to this realization, but having done so, my life has
been forever enriched and transformed. While I am a loyal
Episcopalian and would never leave the church that has nurtured me all my adult life, I readily seek strength and enlightenment from other traditions, Christian and non-Christian
alike.

Several years ago I visited a remarkable church in San Jose, California, called St. Philip's. Composed of five distinct ethnic and cultural congregations within the larger parish, it is considered among the most multicultural churches of my denomination in the nation. Hispanic, Laotian, African American, European American, and Filipino congregations gather at St. Philip's, along with significant numbers of Native Americans, Indians from India, and Pacific Islanders. The various congregations follow their separate meeting schedules, and they also share their unique festivals with the whole congregation: Latinos celebrate the martyrdom of Archbishop Oscar Romero, the Feast of the Three Kings, and Carnival, while African Americans organize a celebration to honor Martin Luther King, Jr., at the new year. The Lao have a new year's festival which includes lighting the candle boats, and the members—some of them former Buddhist monks—intone the ancient chants of the East. The Kirking of the Tartan revives an old American colonial custom linking members of Scottish clans to the Highlands. Bagpipes fill the sanctuary while Scots bring out their various tartans. But at St. Philip's the Kirking of the Tartan has become a festival for all as church members from the other cultures that make up the congregation also bring fabrics from their lands of origin— batiks and prints from Africa, silks of Southeast Asia, alpaca ponchos from Latin America, and tapas from the Pacific. This colorful collection is blessed ("kirked"), and the congregation's members are symbolically linked to their origins and to each other. Each celebration is followed by a feast of cuisine typical of the country or culture being celebrated, so covered dish suppers at St. Philip's are extraordinary culinary events. Once a month the separate congregations join together in one united, glorious festival service.

Icons and symbols on the walls and at tables and side altars at St. Philip's reinforce the cultural traditions of the members. The *Santo Niño* (Holy Child) is an icon important to Filipino members that also speaks to Anglos and Latinos, just as the Virgin of Guadalupe is significant for Mexicans and other

Latin Americans. There is a reclining Buddha and a Lao candle tree. The church sanctuary has seating on four sides to represent the four corners of the world; the Jerusalem cross above the altar draws all people, along with their cultures, traditions, languages, and artifacts, into one human family gathered around the Holy God of the Universe.

The eucharistic prayer is recited in English, Spanish, Lao, and Tagalog, further expressing the reality that although we may come from every corner of the globe, from a multitude of human families and tongues, we are all one holy people of God. To explain the cross-fertilization of religious expressions, one of the priests at St. Philip's, Winifredo (Fred) Veraga, took an image from his native Philippines. It is of the milkfish, which, according to Father Veraga, grows at the borders where fresh and salt water converge. Like the milkfish, he says, our spirituality thrives at the convergence of cultures and traditions. I liked the image but I was skeptical—how can a Buddhist also be a Christian? He replied, "Our Buddhist members remain Buddhist and when they accept Christianity, they are putting on another layer to their spiritual garment." I still remained unconvinced until, quite unexpectedly, I came face-to-face with Buddhism in Japan.

■   ▦   ▦

In Kyoto alone there are some two thousand Shinto and Buddhist temples and shrines, and they are literally everywhere—in residential neighborhoods, on street corners, in commercial areas and markets, along roadways, and especially in places of natural beauty. These may be a pool of fresh water, a waterfall, candles in a dark cave, a shrine in a grove of bamboo trees. There will perhaps be a large brass gong, a basin of cool water with long-handled cups for passersby to take a drink. The shrine may be a graceful arrangement of rocks, or lanterns and prayer boards, a statue of Buddha overlooking a luxuriant landscape. A city shrine may be as simple as a recess carved out of the corner of a modern residential building or a rural shrine as large as a stony outcropping on a mountainside. In the United States and Europe, blaze marks painted on tree trunks and rocks point the hiker up the mountain trail. In Japan, the hiker follows the path from shrine to shrine. As I walked along the streets and through the verdant hills, I sensed the graciousness of the people and the hospitality of the land. A powerful awareness of the holy penetrated my very core. I was privileged to see a Japan sharply different from the high-tech superpower country I had expected. This other Japan was a gift to discover—full of high, lush mountains, crashing waterfalls, and clear streams. This was the Japan of cool forests and luscious tiers of verdant rice paddies, street corner shrines, and urban temples.

On a chilly but sunny day during the Golden Week Festival, a few of us took a little wooden train to the foot of Kurama Mountain. We walked through the pretty village of Kurama, passed over a glistening brook, and went through the vermilion *torii* where the temple path begins. A Japanese temple is more than a building; it is woods, gardens, ponds, waterfalls, streams. It is giant gongs, incense, candles, and prayer boards. It covers anything from a city block to an entire mountain and often mixes Buddhist and Shinto artifacts. As we climbed Kurama Mountain, we passed shrines, some with incense burning, others with water slowly dripping into cool rock basins. Members of the Kurama school of Buddhism believe that six million years ago, Mao-son, the king of the conqueror of evil and the spirit of the earth, descended upon Mount Kurama from Venus to save the earth. In 770 CE a temple was built on the mountain to honor Mao-son—also known as Sonten—and to bear witness to the sacredness of creation.

In the main temple building I came across an explanation of the Sonten trinity in which the spirit of the moon is understood as love, the spirit of the sun as light, and the spirit of the earth as power. Along with it I discovered the "Prayer of Love, Light and Power":

O God, beautiful as the moon, warm as the sun, powerful as the earth, bestow your blessings upon us to
uplift humankind. In this holy place, grant that peace
may defeat discord, unselfishness may conquer greed,
sincere words may overcome deceit, and that respect
may surmount insults. Fill our hearts with joy, uplift
our spirits, and fill our bodies with glory. Great God of
the Universe, Great Light, Great Mover, bestow upon
us who gather to worship you, upon those who strive
to touch your heart, a new strength and glorious light.[3]

The words of this beautiful prayer drove me to the heart of
my Christian faith. It prompted in me an overpowering sense
of God's love and care for all, and of awe at the goodness of
God's creation.

As I continued my walk down the backside of Kurama
Mountain through the thick, dark green bamboo forest, I
knew I was coming down a different person. A door had been
opened. I was filled with an insatiable desire to discover the
wealth of wisdom embedded in other great religions of the
world. In following this path I intuitively knew that my
Christian faith would continue to deepen, and I sensed that I
would arrive at a more global sense of the wonder, the beauty,
the majesty, and the justice of God—the God of a thousand
names and faces. Passing through the temple gate to Mount
Kurama opened my eyes to seek and value wisdom and to
nurture it from wherever it comes. By a random hike I found
myself traveling down a bright new path to enlightenment
that had been trod by many before me. I understood in my
inner being that I could have it all—that there was no need
to reject any religion, philosophy, or source of enlightenment
that nourishes the soul. I learned for myself that I could be
like the Buddhists in Fred Veraga's Christian congregation; I
could add marvelous layers to my spiritual garment.

■   ■   ■

My awakened consciousness also aroused an insatiable desire to experience the treasures of Christian traditions other than my own. For eight years I had the good fortune to live across the pedestrian walkway from one of the finest Roman Catholic churches in France, St. Gervais. This lovely, historic church is the home of the monastic Communities of Jerusalem, a relatively new monastic community of men and women that was founded in 1975. The community of about a hundred brothers and sisters in Paris (actually the order is much larger, with other communities in Vezelay, Mont-Saint-Michel, and Florence) believes that God is revealed through a life of work in the heart of the world, through contemplation and prayer in the contradictions and complexities of the urban setting. Influenced by Charles de Foucauld, who lived a monastic life in the desert of Algeria, the community wanted to create an oasis in the urban desert of Paris, where there is so much pain, competition, and indifference.

Like most city dwellers, members of the community rent their housing; they work as wage-earners in the neighborhood; they embrace the rhythms of the city—and morning, noon, and night they gather in the church for the most exquisite liturgies I have experienced anywhere. When I was at home in Paris, I never failed to attend the daily 6:30 evening Eucharist, along with the several hundred others who, like me, would not willfully miss a service. We were attracted by the deep spirituality of the community of the young brothers and sisters, by the sincerity of their prayer and the simple reading of the scriptures, by their heartfelt singing, by the warmth of the passing of the peace and their welcome to us. When we would sing, in French, "Drop, drop, drop all the worries of the world," for this moment of prayer, I did just that. When the brothers and sisters offered the bread and wine, I truly felt as if I was receiving the sacred meal of Christ, that I was a privileged guest at his heavenly banquet, at one with the community and with so many of my Paris neighbors. I felt at one with the generations of the faithful who had worshiped at this place, and I left every night invigorated for the journey.

I was raised a Roman Catholic but left the Catholic Church as a teenager. I almost never went anywhere near a Catholic church until I discovered St. Gervais! When I did, it was like a homecoming, like the tender embrace of relatives who had come back into my life after many years away. I felt like Humpty Dumpty, as the two Christian traditions that have been so influential to me were finally put together. I suppose that most church authorities would say that I should pick one of my churches—Catholic or Protestant—and stick with it. I have heard this approach disdainfully referred to as a "supermarket approach to religion," but I do not feel that way. I believe that I can have and cherish both of my traditions, and furthermore that the way is open to me—and to all of us—to be fed by other religions and philosophies very different from the ones of our birth.

▪ ▪ ▪

There is no reason to reject any authentic channel that brings life, spirit, and vitality, and the good news is that we *can* have it all. For me, this has meant being shaped and informed by the spiritual treasures of several traditions, such as the *Dhammapada,* which is rightly considered one of the great masterpieces of world religious writing. This Buddhist work is practical and straightforward, and when I have been very angry or distressed, or when I have felt as if I needed to get my emotions under control, there is nothing more direct than the simple words of the *Dhammapada* that remind me that "our life is shaped by our mind; we become what we think. . . . Joy follows a pure thought like a shadow that never leaves."[4]

Since that first trip to Japan I have met people of many varieties of religious traditions. I have had the pleasure of meeting Orthodox Christians in Romania and Albania, where I have been entranced by the beauty of their churches, their candles, their glittering sanctuaries and commanding icons. And while I may not have appreciated the muezzin's dawn call to prayer from the mosque next to where I was staying in Tirana, I was always moved by the Muslim faithful, who at certain appointed times of day stop everything, unroll their rugs, face Mecca, and fall prostrate in prayer. During the first Iraq War my husband and I were welcomed to a beautiful mosque located at the tip of Gibraltar. Although the symbolism of the new mosque built right on one of the Pillars of Hercules, the narrowest opening of the Mediterranean that cuts its way between Africa and Europe, was not lost on us, we nonetheless admired the beauty of the house of worship and the hospitality of the people.

The truth that was unfolded to me on Kurama Mountain is that my own Christian faith is deepened and strengthened by encounters with other traditions. They bring me to the essence of my own tradition. "What is essential for Christian faith," according to Joseph C. Hough, Jr., the president of Union Theological Seminary in New York, "is that we know we have seen the face of God in the love of Jesus Christ. It is not essential to believe that no one else has seen God and experienced redemption in another time and place."[5]

When we were building a brick wall and chimney in our house to accommodate a wood-burning stove, our stonemason suggested that maybe a small brick mantelpiece would look nice behind the stove. Yes, we thought, our mantelpiece would be our *tokonoma*. In Japan almost every home, however simple, has a *tokonoma*—an alcove, usually illuminated by soft indirect lighting, in which is arranged something of beauty or imagination: a simple flower arrangement, a single, tall branch in a slim vase, a few stones artfully positioned, driftwood. The arrangement is generally small, and the appearance is one of both beauty and starkness. In a Japanese home the *tokonoma* is a place of calm in what may be a busy household, inviting householders to stop a moment and perhaps offer a fleeting prayer. Our *tokonoma* holds several icons: a vibrantly colored Salvadoran cross, small triptychs—one

German and the other Salvadoran—depicting the nativity. These are all gifts from friends. The most recent addition is a tiny beadwork turtle—symbol of long life—given to me by a Lakota woman, Dottie LeBeau, who was my neighbor in a tiny hamlet on the Rosebud Reservation in South Dakota many years ago. In front of these various artifacts we have votive candles, which we light whenever we have a special prayer, a friend who is ill perhaps, thanksgiving for the birth of a baby, for family members who are traveling, or when we just want to thank God for a beautiful day. Throughout the day the *tokonoma,* situated in the warm center of our house, is an ever-present reminder of God's presence with us—the God of a thousand names and faces who is with us every moment of our lives. And in the evening when the shadows have fallen and the stove is cooling and we are getting ready to drift off to bed, we sit in front of it to say our evening prayers.

We feel and meet God through a myriad of channels throughout our lives. For me the pungent scent of burning sage, the hollow, mellow voice of a gong, the cry of the ram's horn, and the call of the minaret now join with the bells of the Angelus summoning us to prayer and reverence for all people and cultures on the earth.

3

Work:
The Fabric of the World

Workers keep stable the fabric of the world, and their
prayer is in the practice of their trade.

—Ecclesiasticus 38:34

I was a doctoral student with an academic husband just
beginning his career, and the mother of three young children.
I needed to make money any way I could. On a day that had
been like every other day for the previous nine months, I got
a flash of insight into what I and everyone else on earth were
doing. Stuck in traffic on Dixwell Avenue at 8:30 in the
morning, inching my way along to my dead-end job as a
receptionist at Administrative Data Systems, *I was going to
work.* It was a bitterly cold morning, and the exhaust of
countless vehicles froze as it circled the traffic jam. Hunkered
down inside their warm cars the people around me were listening to their radios as they sipped their coffee and ate their
breakfast; they were writing shopping lists and thinking about
what they had to do at work, who they were going to see,
what they had planned afterward. I could hear an occasional
muffled tune escaping from a car or two, and I observed fingers on steering wheels beating out the music. And it struck
me powerfully that such is the music of life. This is the historic project of human beings, going and coming from work

today and every day. In the words of Ecclesiasticus, "Without them a city cannot be built.... They keep stable the fabric of the world" (38:32, 34).

Work is a fundamental dimension of human experience—indeed, the experience of all beings. The psalmist says, "People go out to their work and to their labor until the evening" (Psalm 104:23). The mother rises before dawn, showers, dresses, and applies her makeup. She wakes her children, prepares their breakfast, packs their lunch boxes, and drops them off at the daycare center. She's tired before her workday has begun; nonetheless, she takes a deep breath and heads for the interstate and another day at the office. The swan gathers twigs to build a nest for her young. After the birth of her cygnets she will spend her days feeding and training them until they can take care of themselves and fly off. When that day comes, the female swan will again gather the twigs as she continues her work of building the nest for the new generation.

God creates. Human beings, made in the image of God, carry on the task of creating the world. The creation story is a whirlwind of the awesome creativity of God, but God does not complete it. The role of human beings is to continue where God leaves off, and this is done mainly through human labor, through people going to work every day. On the eighth day, we pick up the task of creation. A woman takes up her shovel and basket of seeds and goes out to sow her field. A man hunts for food and builds dwellings and shelters; they will birth their children and tend their flocks—tasks that continue from morning till evening, day in and day out, for weeks and months and years. Thus the eighth day continues as we human beings take our places in the continuous cycles of creation which God has ordained from the first syllable of time. In the encyclical *On Human Work,* Pope John Paul II stated that human beings work because God works and that the work of men and women reflects that of their Creator. In the words of the encyclical, "Every human reflects the very action of the creator of the universe."[6] So through work, human beings continue God's creativity in the world, and indeed become co-creators with God, caring for and sustaining the world.

St. Thomas Aquinas said that there can be no joy in life without joy in work. Sigmund Freud, when questioned about the basic criteria for mental health, answered, "To love and to work."Yet the annals of history also suggest the complexity of work and its two-edged sword: that work is both a curse and a blessing; that work has brought injustice and oppression. Hard work has been associated with virtue; it has also cruelly divided the human family. Historically, the status that workers enjoy rises the less they make their livelihood with their hands. The paper pusher in an office has more status than the broom pusher on the evening cleaning crew; the lawyer's work is more highly regarded than the construction worker's. Brain work trumps physical work. Long after my father's death, I discovered his family's Bible, and in it I was moved by the stark listing of a certain John Wheeler who had lost his life building the railroad in Chicago. Indeed, many of our grand-parents and great-grandparents toiled away in Lower East Side sweatshops or built railroads like my great uncle, or con-structed urban office buildings or paved interstate highways, hoping all the time that their children would never have to feed a machine on a noisy, hot assembly line, stitch clothing together in a garment factory, hurl steel and lumber and rail-road ties, or ever have to raise a hammer in order to put bread on the family dining table. One part of us wants to forget how our forebears earned their livelihood; another part wants to remember and even to admire.

Around the time I was working in my dead-end recep-tionist job, I came across an article about United States Senator Bob Graham who, as a young member of the Florida Senate, was involved in education issues. He was challenged by teachers who told him that if he really wanted to find out what was happening in education, he should spend time in the classroom. He did, teaching history at Carol City High School near Miami. That was thirty years ago, and Graham was so impressed by the value of firsthand knowledge that he started taking different jobs around the state, one a month. Graham has poured cement on the deck of a new bridge in Tampa, and he has been on the cleanup crew at the Orange Bowl. He's been a farm worker, security officer, flight attendant, forest ranger, citrus packer for Tropicana, a construction worker of the Daytona International Speedway, assembly line worker, cargo inspector, and bank teller in Vero Beach. When Graham had completed three hundred and sixty-five days of work, he celebrated with his fellow employees at US Airways, where he was working as a flight attendant, customer service agent, and baggage handler on the Tallahassee-Tampa-Miami route. "If you want to find out about people," he said, "what they're thinking, their hopes, their dreams, their problems—there's no better way than to work with them."[7] Through all these jobs he got to the heart of the meaning of human work and its significance in the lives of his constituents.

As I drove back and forth down Dixwell Avenue every day in all sorts of weather conditions, I kept thinking about the fact that if human work is at the center of the human project on earth, then there must be some relationship between work and the development of my spiritual life. I asked myself how my work with computer programmers and managers, with greeting guests in the office, with typing letters and reports could possibly be considered prayer. Then I made what, to me, was a revelatory discovery in the book of Ecclesiasticus: a laborer's work is, in fact, a *prayer.* The thirty-eighth chapter of Ecclesiasticus speaks of the wisdom of the plowman, the crafter, the artisan, the smith, and the potter, who set their hearts upon finishing their handiwork:

> All these rely on their hands,
>   and each is skillful in their own work.
> Without them a city cannot be established,
>   and people can neither sojourn nor live there. . . .
> They keep stable the fabric of the world,
>   and *their prayer is in the practice of their trade.*
>   (Ecclesiasticus 38:31–32, 34)

■ ■ ■

I finished my receptionist job at the computer office, completed my Ph.D., wrote *The Liberation of the Laity,* and started teaching a course at the Hartford Theological Seminary called Ministry in Daily Life. Influenced both by the insights of Senator Graham and some of my own, I thought the class would be a good way to test my sense that people live out their calling in their jobs. At the least it would give my students, who were pastors of various denominations, the opportunity to learn about the real world of their church members and discover how they seek to live out their faith on the job. Over the semester, each student had to visit four members of their congregation at their places of employment. I asked them to use their imaginations and select "work mentors" from a variety of employment areas: hourly wage earners, professionals, people employed in health care, and those in public life. I asked that work mentors represent a cross section of the congregation: men and women, "blue collar" workers, managers, teachers, artists, and mechanics, those who work in the trades, people who are self-employed, workers in small and large companies. I told them, "You will need to 'shadow' your work mentors in their work long enough to get some sense of the principalities and powers, angels and devils, temptations and supports, challenges and frustrations, skills and inadequacies, assumptions and dilemmas of workplaces visited. How does your work mentor relate to other individuals in the workplace? Can the individual affect the workplace or institution for the better?"

As I described the assignment, I could feel the level of anxiety rising: "I wouldn't want to impose on my parishioners, they lead such busy lives. . . . I don't have the time to spend a whole day at someone's office. . . . Can I write a paper instead?" Clearly the prospect of pastors asking for the help of their congregants made them nervous, and they just did not want to do it. I coaxed and cajoled and humored them, and finally I compromised and told them to try one visit before the next class.

Next week there was such a buzz of animated conversation among the students, they hardly noticed my arrival. Calling them to attention, I asked them how their visits had gone. Dave Koppel, who had visited his congregant Tom in a factory that makes small metal parts in Waterbury, said, "I was surprised to find that Tom is a toolmaker. I expected to find him operating a machine. I am impressed by the knowledge and skill he possesses, and I realize that I (and all of us) depend on Tom and people like him to provide us with so many things we use every day. It's amazing to think of how interdependent we all are."

Geordie Campbell went to work with another toolmaker. His parishioner, Whitey, owns a small tool company with fifty employees that his father began forty years ago. They manufacture gauges that measure the tolerances of screw threads. Pretty ordinary, nondescript work, Geordie thought—until he considered its implications. One of the gauges the company manufactures tests the threads of the universal joint that holds a Boeing 747 together. Geordie said after his visit, "I will never fly in a plane again without being grateful for the hours spent making the gauges that provide standards for the engine, the wheels, and even the screws that hold the sheet metal on the wings."

These two pastor/students, with merely one visit to a place of daily work, had come away with valuable insights. Our health and well-being depend upon the strength of the nuts and bolts keeping aircraft together in the sky and vehicles overland intact, but this is not something to which we give much thought. Furthermore, even one short visit to a parishioner's workplace changed several of the students' views of ministry. Warren Bouton went to work with Dick, who is the statewide manager of a company that installs traffic lights. At the conclusion of the day, Warren admitted that before this he had thought most ministry was done through the church:

"Certainly laypeople had ministries, but that meant through the committees of the church, through nonprofit organizations, through structures designated as ministry. My visit with Dick introduced an entirely new concept of Christ's service. To be honest, it's so obvious, practical, and logical that it's almost embarrassing to admit!"

Martin Montonye went to work with Maureen, a registered nurse who supervises a cardiothoracic intensive care unit at a large New Haven hospital. "Watching Maureen and other staff members perform their duties made me aware that they must be in touch with their faith, and trust their faith. This visit shattered my unconscious assumption that only 'real' ministers did 'real' ministry. I never thought I would say something like this, because I truly believed I thought otherwise—that is, until I made this visit and observed firsthand someone doing 'real' ministry in another setting defined as a medical facility. In fact, I'm even a bit envious of her."

The course was up and running. Over the ensuing five months the students eagerly went to work with a telephone technician, two police officers, a computer technician, a home inspector, three teachers, a counselor in a women's prison, a veterinarian, an auto mechanic, four nurses, a social worker, the president of a company that distributes office machinery, an enforcement officer for the State of Connecticut Environmental Protection Agency, a software salesman, a shipping clerk, a plumber, a school food service manager, a bagger at a supermarket, a Greyhound bus driver, an insurance underwriter, a mortgage officer, an electrical engineer, a technician in an environmental analysis laboratory, a professional singer, and two toolmakers. I had only an inkling that these pastor-students could benefit from visiting their parishioners at work; I had not expected what amounted to a conversion. They got a short course on the spiritual significance of daily work and, as they did, discovered the truth captured by William Conrad, the owner of a small business, when he said, "Work for me is my major connection with life on earth."

This small group of students sent me on my own journey of discovery to talk to as many workers as I could to try to understand how they see themselves seeking and following God through the ordinary channels of their lives. I met Marion Ridley, a surgeon in Tampa, who told me, "I meet Christ in a lot of people. People bear their souls to me. I can feel the dignity and worth of every person. . . . It is always an inspiration to me to see the human spirit and how resilient it is, to see how it can be down and how it can rise up out of ashes." A commercial fisherman, Edward Todd, of Point Judith, Rhode Island, owns an eighty-foot trawler that he operates with three crew members. Most of his trips are for two to five days, and he goes to places such as the "Dump," the "Fingers," and the "Fishtail," so called because of their shapes on the nautical map. "You know there is something else bigger than you when you look out at the ocean—the majesty of it, the sheer power," he said. "Sometimes we thought we were going to meet God coming home in a storm at night!" Other times the presence of God is experienced at sea even more dramatically, "The first time I took my son to George's Bank, we were just coming out of Nantucket Sound, just past the last set of buoys, and we saw a rainbow. I mean we saw both ends of it, and we sailed right under it. The colors were so vivid. I saw God at that moment."

■   ■   ■

Though rarely articulated, many if not most of us intuitively understand that we live out our faith through our daily work and that our daily work is our prayer. It is a gift already in our hands, a cornucopia of spiritual treasures just waiting to be opened. Our work is an opportunity for self-expression, a process as well as a product, a bridge to extend the sacred to the world of the ordinary. We can practice justice through the regular channels of our work, by our attitudes to others, by how we treat our employees and employers, by our speaking up and speaking out, and by the decisions we make, both small and large. Our work keeps stable the fabric of society, and our work continues the work of creation. Through each of these avenues we build and enrich ourselves, we keep God's world sound and safe, and we extend the realm of the sacred as we make all ground holy ground.

What personal needs does our work fulfill for us? Jessica Wilson is a librarian in Narragansett, Rhode Island. "I enjoy being around books and helping people have access to what they want," she says. "I like having a job where I can make a little child feel she can fit in and make a contribution. I feel that in so many ways children aren't able to get involved. I like to go with a child's rhythm. I like having them feel that adults will respond to them. I like to include everybody and have everybody recognized. It is this recognizing and including everybody that makes me see God." Work like Jessica's allows for human fulfillment and respect. It is work that builds up and enriches.

Our work is a process just as much as it is a product. To see this is essential, since so much work is soon undone or has no tangible result at all. When work is seen as process, workers "make" themselves through the faithfulness of the work. The potter makes a beautiful bowl and shapes herself in the process; the cabinetmaker builds himself while he is crafting the cupboard and fitting in its drawers. Jim Cunningham is a carpenter who came to build bookcases for our immense collection of books. Young then and a little shy, he would simply make a rough calculation of the cost of materials on a scrap of wood and hand it to us. Jim took hours building them, concentrating as he fitted the boards in place, getting so lost in his work he would be surprised when I would ask him if he knew how late it was. Upon finishing a job, Jim steps back to behold—and yes—even to admire it. He loves wood, and he can make any wood floor or bookcase or barn or deck look like a work of art. Even shingles and roofs and doors and windows have that special quality of having been built with care. Jim's work is a product, of course, but through it he also "builds" himself and increases his skill as he faithfully goes about his tasks.

Our work is a bridge to extend the sacred to the world of the ordinary. The challenge is to come to an appreciation of how we are faithful and how we find God through the ordinary channels of our lives, not apart from them. We convey God's love and God's justice, God's caring for the dignity of every individual, wherever we are. As seekers trying to be faithful to God at every moment of our lives, we have no more compelling task as a people than to see the holy all around us. Therefore, the workplaces where we are physically present during the week are of utmost importance in crafting a spirituality of everyday work.

■ ■ ■

God's peace, God's love, and God's justice are intended to be mediated through the lives of ordinary people engaged in the ordinary responsibilities of our lives. We do justice as we move along in our jobs, not apart from them, whether we are diplomats, factory workers, farmers, computer technicians, software designers, department store clerks, or chefs. Traditional good works of mercy and outreach are important but secondary to the living out of God's love and God's justice through the ordinary channels of daily work. Oscar Romero, the martyred archbishop of El Salvador, said, "Let each of you, in your own job, in your vocation—nun, married person, bishop, priest, high school or university student, workman, laborer, market woman—each of you in your own place live the faith so intensely and feel that in your surroundings you are a true microphone of God our Lord."[8] In doing so, we extend the realm of the secular so that all ground is holy ground and every location a hallowed place.

People of faith "keep stable the fabric of the world" through work that contributes to keeping the structures of the world healthy and safe. A spirituality of the fabric will find expression in occupations which, unless you are employed in them, you may never even think about: civil engineers, air traffic controllers, long-distance truck drivers, road crews, sanitation workers, maids and office cleaners, utility workers. My model for one who has a ministry that keeps stable the fabric of society is my friend Charlie Smith, who repairs the engines of the town's heavy road machinery and fixes trucks of all kinds. Much of his work is done in the still hours of the morning while most of the townspeople sleep. When the snowfall is heavy and skilled drivers are needed, Charlie is out there plowing the streets. Were it not for the fact that Charlie was a member of the same church I used to attend, I would probably remain oblivious to his work, and I would probably take clear, clean streets in a snowy winter for granted. Because of Charlie and all the other Charlies who are out there plowing the streets in the early hours on snowy mornings, children get to school safely and their parents are able to get to their offices. His work keeps stable the fabric of society.

In Atlanta I met Ed, whose job is to walk four miles of MARTA tracks every morning. He checks for debris on these tracks of the city's public transportation, and identifies anything that does not look right. By the time the cars begin rolling, every track of the system has been walked by Ed and his colleagues, who have made sure that the system is safe for another day. Do Charlie and Ed see their work as holy work? Ed certainly does, for when I questioned him he said, "Why, sure. The system works safely because I check it. There are no accidents because I have cleared the tracks." Such a broad spirituality teaches us to appreciate those necessary but largely invisible works that are essential to the smooth running of public life.

■   ■   ■

Work at its best takes raw nature and shapes it to meet human needs and the needs of God's precious creation. I live in the woodlands of eastern Connecticut, a land full of rocks. The nature preserve where I take my daily hike is full of fieldstone walls and ancient rock foundations where the wooden houses and barns have long disappeared. I marvel at the strength of the early farmers who cleared this land of rocks. The rocks not only made beautiful and functional divisions between fields, but their removal made the land tillable. Rocks become dry walls. Rushing water becomes hydroelectric power. Sun and wind and the movement of tides become heat and energy. Forests become homes, natural iron in the earth becomes steel, nature's herbs and plants become drugs for healing, raw materials of human creativity become books, paintings, sculptures, surgical procedures. Grapes become the wine of the Eucharist, wheat is transformed into the bread of heaven. Dorothy Day once said, "We are co-creators with God by our responsible acts, whether in bringing forth children, producing food or making clothing." Through our work we become co-creators with God. God creates through us, the people of God.

In the most basic way, people follow Jesus through their being—their thoughts, attitudes, ideas, feelings; through their bearing and believing. Spirituality encompasses being. Perhaps the job is tedious and routine—many people literally detest their jobs, and much of our work is unsatisfying, unrewarding, unexciting, taken on out of necessity. But even if our jobs are drudgery, we commonly spend many hours each day with our companion workers, hours that add up to weeks, months, and years. Our companion employees have babies, family weddings, and funerals; they get divorced, win at the casino, and lose in the state lottery. Their children get arrested for drunk driving; they graduate from college; they get their first jobs. They get thrown out of apartments, they make foolish mistakes, they spend too much money. These people with whom we work represent every stage of life, every age, every human activity, every passion, all of life's joys and failings; they are part of every aspect of God's creation.

Jesus came to work among us. Isn't this the meaning of the incarnation? God comes to us through Jim Cunningham, the carpenter, and Charlie Smith, the heavy equipment mechanic; through toolmakers and surgeons like Marion Ridley; through building inspectors; through librarians like Jessica Wilson; through secretaries, teachers, pilots, software designers, dentists, lawyers, and the unemployed waiting in line at the benefits office; through the worker at the adjoining desk; through the busy waitress who takes time to smile at the lunchtime diner. God comes to us through Ed Todd, the commercial fisherman who sees God as he sails his trawler under a dazzling rainbow. God makes all ground holy. God hallows us, and God hallows the eighth day. Ordinary work is an arena where faith is lived out. In *To Work and To Love: A Theology of Creation,* Dorothee Soelle writes,

> It is through our most human activities, in work and in love, that we become co-creators of the new earth, the place we all call home. . . . We may join Jesus in understanding that work is the way in which we are personally involved in God's ongoing creation and the redemption of the world.[9]

All we need to live passionately is to unwrap the gifts already in our hands. Our daily work is such a gift. Open it.

4

Cherishing Children

*It's very important for all of us to understand the oppor-
tunity a child presents to us, but also what a moral challenge a child is to us. Are we going to do justice to this
new life?*

—Robert Coles, *Listening to Children: A Moral Journey*

Red and wrinkled with a head full of damp black hair and a
furrowed brow, Virginia was forty-five minutes old. I held my
first child close, admiring a little person that only a mother
could consider beautiful. She wiggled and squirmed, stretched
her arms and splayed her tiny fingers as she released a squeaky
cry. Giving her the breast brought instant calm as Virginia
tugged at the nipple, sucking down her first meal as I realized
that from this moment on, my life would be forever changed.
It would never be quite the way it was even the day before,
when she was still a heavy bulge inside. The realization struck
me sharply that this hungry seven-and-a-half-pounder—this
little stranger at my breast—would have a lot to teach me, and
I her.

Virginia was born in the mid-1960s in an old-fashioned
maternity home—*not a hospital,* my British neighbors
insisted; hospitals are for the sick—with the quaint name of
the British Home for Mothers and Babies. My ward was a
large room where twelve new mothers with their babies nes-
tled in little cribs beside their beds. We were together as if we

were in one big family. We got to know each other because
the founders of the British Home felt that new mothers
needed to stay for ten days in order to rest and learn how to
care for their babies. And learn we did! All day long grandmothers from this Southeast London borough of Woolwich
would come and go and teach us how to change and bathe
our babies, how to feed them, how to "burp" them. "Pin the
nappy, not the baby." "Hold her this way, love." "Support her
neck when you feed her." "Test the heat of the water before
you put your baby in it." During all their instruction these
no-nonsense grannies stressed that nurturing is natural, and
when we were in doubt all we had to do was remember to
trust our instincts and common sense, just as women throughout every age have always done.

In a sense, Virginia was not my first child. I had been a
fifth- and sixth-grade teacher at a school for Native American
girls in Springfield, South Dakota, and a high school English
and history teacher at a huge London comprehensive school,
equivalent to an American high school. Before that I had
taught Bible school on the Rosebud and Standing Rock
reservations of South Dakota and in the Mission District of
San Francisco. I believed then, and I still do, that cherishing
and nurturing children is natural to all human beings whether
they be birth parents or not, and that a basic element of our
nature is to protect, teach, and guide the next generation,
thereby ensuring the survival of human life on earth. This is a
natural, God-given inclination whatever our age or condi-
tion. Examples of this abound: my friend Chester Cooke has
neither spouse nor children but he has many godchildren, and
he has taken an interest and guided a generation of music students at the Yale Institute of Sacred Music. Now that he lives
in Maine, Chester takes enormous pleasure in providing a
home away from home for two Canadian hockey players and
their friends who are students at Bowdoin College.

Dorothy and Worth Campbell also have godchildren and
many other young people whom they have loved, guided, and
educated from youth to adulthood. "Not having our own

children has given us more time and occasion to be with a whole range of young people whom we feel very close to," Worth remarked recently. When Worth celebrated his seventy-fifth birthday, all thirteen godchildren along with their spouses, partners, and children were invited to a celebration at the Campbells' home on Cape Cod. There were fifty in all, two from France and one who lives in Germany. Thinking back on their lives of nurturing the young, Worth said, "For us, being godparents and friends with young people has given us a sense of vocation. We were doing something that was a privilege to share in. I feel that ours has been a variant of the vocation to nurture that all blood parents have." Now Worth has pancreatic cancer and does not know much longer he will live—perhaps a year, maybe less. Most of the godchildren and other young friends from all over have visited the Campbells to bid him farewell. One young man who came from Uganda told them, "You have been true parents to me."

To cherish and nurture children is truly to serve God. As Jesus tells us, "Whoever welcomes one such child in my name welcomes me" (Matt. 18:5). Nurturing the young draws from the depth of our humanity, and our children become our teachers as we become theirs. What then do children teach us?

▪   ▪   ▪

Children teach us first of all that we are all part of the continuity of life and the flow of generations. Because of children, the human family on earth continues until the next generation and the next. Just as our grandmothers raised our parents and our parents brought us up and gave us food for the journey of life, so we guide and protect the little ones we have in our care right now. So this has been, and so it will be until the last syllable of recorded time.

Children also teach us to grow up, become responsible, and put selfishness aside. My newborn daughter needed to be fed every four hours, whether I felt like it or not. She made it easy for me to grow up because her arrival into our lives evoked a deep love that made it natural to feed and protect her and later to guide her. Here was someone in my life more valuable than myself, someone I would go to the ends of the earth to save and protect, someone I would die for. Children give us a second chance to encounter and enjoy the pleasures of childhood. They give the child in us a second chance to spend long weekend days building sand castles and riding an inner tube down a lazy river, going to the circus, riding the wave, visiting the doll museum, taking the Staten Island Ferry, exploring aquariums and science museums, reptile gardens and dinosaur exhibits. Children give their parents the chance to revel in snow days—sledding down the hill in the back of the house, going ice skating, building snowmen, and lying on the newly fallen snow to carve snow angels. Because of children we go camping and tell stories around the campfire while we imagine a midnight visit of a grizzly bear. Children give us a second chance to make Christmas cookies, to draw pictures and make card houses, to win and lose at chess and checkers. They give us a second chance to tell outrageous stories, to make up rhymes and jingles, to laugh at silly jokes. They give us a reason to read again children's classics and even some new ones like the Harry Potter books. Children take us to carnivals and fairs and Fourth of July fireworks. With them we relish cotton candy and taffy apples, hot dogs and corn dogs and marshmallows on a stick. They take us to puppet shows and ballets, to music in the park, to parades and picnics. They take us canoeing, tumbling down water slides, and hiking up mountains, screaming as the roller coaster descends from its height and gazing at the heavens on a starry night, following the planets in their courses.

Children teach us wonder, as Sam Keen said so beautifully in *Apology for Wonder:*

> Wonder in the child is the capacity for sustained and continued delight, marvel, amazement and enjoyment. It is the capacity of the child to approach the world as if it were a smorgasbord of potential delights, waiting to

be tasted. . . . To wonder is to live in a world of novelty
rather than law, of delight rather than obligation, and of
the present rather than the future.[10]

My husband and I were given a short course in wonder by our
nephews, eight and ten, when we were together on Ile St.
Honorat, a short ferry ride from Cannes in the Mediterranean.
After a few hours of swimming and snorkeling in the
turquoise water on the west of the island, we took a short walk
to the monastery where St. Augustine and St. Patrick are said
to have stayed. When we entered the cool, dark chapel the
boys were suddenly quiet. They peered at the stained-glass
windows and the flickering votive candles. Then Ashley
remarked, "I can hear the angels." We enquired as to what he
meant and he said, "Listen. You have to be very quiet. You
can't see the angels but they are here. You can feel them. It is
God talking to us." Through them we understood the wisdom
of Dorothee Soelle, who said, "Children and artists are teachers of spirituality of creation. They recombine created things
into a new synthesis, and they change triviality into wonder,
givenness into createdness. Through them we un-learn triviality and learn amazement, we again see the magnolia tree,
and we see it for the first time."[11]

Children can even show us how to accept reality and loss.
Dixie, a fierce-looking Husky and German shepherd mix, was
a gentle creature. The children played hide-and-seek with her,
they tried to ride her, and they snuggled in her furry coat. She
was a part of the household when Anna was born, and it
seemed as if she would be there forever. Anna was five when
Dixie became ill and died. Her parents discussed at great
length just how they should break the news to Anna that her
beloved dog and playmate had died. They decided to tell her
the truth and, to their surprise, Anna accepted it without
question. She was sad, but said she knew that "Dixie is in
heaven, where everyone goes who gets so sick they can't get
better. She is in heaven with the angels and Katie O'Grady's
grandmother." Just like that.

Children are idealists, and they teach us to hope for and work for a better world. Whenever I am with groups of young people, I try to take time to ask them about their hopes and fears for the future as we continue in this new millennium. I have talked to children across the United States, in the European Community, and in Eastern Europe. Wherever they come from, they are invariably worried about the state of the environment and about war. As part of the United Nations Environmental Program, two thousand children in sixty countries were asked what a better world would look like. Just after the civil war in the former Yugoslavia, a small group of children offered their hopes and dreams:

> I want a world of peace because I hate everything that is not peace. I want a world in which all countries unite. And that united world will be good because no one thinks only of themselves.

> I would like the world to be the most beautiful rainbow. Everything would be clean; knowledge would be falling like rain. When the drops of knowledge touch the ground, they would sparkle in a thousand rainbow colors.

> I want to run, smile and enjoy the beauty of nature in a wonderful, happy world of the future. And we children will make our planet look as we would like it to be—shiny, happy, full of joy and beauty. I want to be friends with the earth, and the sun, the seas and the forests.

> I want the world to look like a nice place where there is no war and no hate, where people like each other, where children are not hungry and naked, where animals are not hunted, where we can travel without fear of being murdered by a crazy terrorist.[12]

Children and young people feel the pain of the world, and too often they suffer from its abuses and injustices. Many chil-

dren in developing nations at war are forced to carry
weapons; many more are downtrodden and abused. Just so
long as hope remains alive in them, they can inspire us. They
can even set us on our life's path. Robert Coles, the Pulitzer
Prize–winning child psychiatrist, was changed forever by a
six-year-old named Ruby Bridges. On his way to a medical
meeting in New Orleans, he happened upon a mob scene in
front of an elementary school during the integration struggles
of the early 1960s, when enraged white men and women
shouted threats and waved placards bearing messages of hate.
To his shock, Coles saw a little girl all dressed up in gleaming
patent-leather shoes and a new dress walking up the school
steps between two federal marshals. It was the first day of
school, and Ruby was the first child of color to attend. When
he later visited Ruby at home and asked what she had said to
the screaming mob, she told him she was praying for them.
"They have so much hate, I have to pray for them because
they don't know what they're doing."[13] Because of her,
Coles's professional career became one of interviewing thousands of children from different races and cultures, from the
very poor to the affluent, listening to their thoughts and fears,
their hearts' desires, and their ideals. Thirty years later Coles
said that Ruby taught him how she and other children who
integrated schools exhibited courage under stress, how they
endured pain, heckling, and ostracization for a larger purpose.

Children widen our horizons and show us new worlds. I
thought I was a sophisticated traveler, confident I could get
along anywhere with a little bit of daring and a lot of imagination—and then I went to Japan to visit my son. Chris walks
confidently down the streets of Kyoto, the ancient Japanese
city of two thousand temples and shrines where he has lived
for a dozen years. Without his help I could not order even the
simplest meal or take a local bus. But Chris opened up to me
a new world where I soon learned how people can live simply in small urban spaces and how they honor and respect
each other. I was introduced to the simple delights of washing
at the community bath, the *sento,* along with his neighbors, and

hiking along the trails leading to the mountains surrounding the city. My first visit to France came about when my son Perry was teaching English in a Parisian high school. I visited Virginia as a Peace Corps volunteer on a remote Marshall Islands atoll, and again when she moved to Nicaragua, and then to Uruguay.

On each occasion our children have opened up new worlds to us. Because of their language skills and their passion for living in cultures very different from their own, we have had the pleasure of meeting local people who have a diversity of values and viewpoints, and who implicitly make us question standard American values while their examples urge us to do what we can to enrich them. But we do not have to have traveling children to have our eyes opened to see new worlds. We learn as much from our children who stay closer to home because, by virtue of their age, they live in a different world than we do. They encounter values and people very different from those of their parents. Our children will become their elders' teachers, if we have the grace to open up and to listen carefully.

■   ■   ■

We elders also have a critical role in cherishing and nurturing our children as parents and teachers, friends, coaches, neighbors, and community members. As Robert Coles asks, "Are we going to do justice to this new life?" We teach children the knowledge that each one of them is loved and valued by everything we do from the moment of birth. We teach by our manner—how we hold our children, how we stroke her head, how we cuddle and smile at him, how we soothe her when she cries, how we laugh and sing with him, how we recite jingles and nursery rhymes. As our children mature, we introduce them to our own enjoyments and interests while supporting theirs. We affirm them simply when we have fun with them, through all those dinner table conversations and chatter that fills a household, and also by welcoming their own friends into our homes.

We give children a sense of place. Every child is born into a family. It may be a conventional family, a single-parent family, an extended family, or anything in between; it may be a family whose home is where generations of the family have lived or it may be a migrant family that follows the crops from south to north. Into whatever circumstances our children are born, they will learn a sense of place by their closeness to their primary caregivers. They will learn that their place is secure with these adults who will protect them.

My grandson Nathaniel had his first day of school in Montevideo, Uruguay. He is the smallest and youngest boy in his kindergarten and the only American child in the class where he has no friends. At recess he tried to play in the "Kids' House," but three boys who are larger than he is would not let him near it. Nathaniel might have retreated into a corner and cried, but he had enough sense of place within himself to be unfazed. No doubt he will soon make it into the Kids' House and make his place in his new school; for the time being, Nathaniel's parents have done a good job in giving him a sense of place in his family along with the strength to deal with his temporary lack of it.

We teach children our values and traditions. A basic sense of fairness and justice is communicated by parents and caregivers; we illustrate by our example the difference between right and wrong, the difference between acceptable and unacceptable behavior. We teach generosity by being generous, consideration by being considerate; we teach our children how to share by the sharing of ourselves. We affirm the value of our own culture by being the storytellers within our family that links generation to generation. At the same time we affirm the diversity of other cultures by the diversity of our friends and associates and affections.

We are responsible caregivers when we acknowledge the painful social and economic divisions in the world and let our children know that such injustice is not acceptable. Our children learn from us when we take action against injustice and invite them to join us. When Christopher Allen-Doucot of Hartford, Connecticut, considered taking his twelve-year-old son Micah on a humanitarian mission to Darfur, Sudan, where the civil war has been going on for two decades, some of their friends worried that the situation was too dangerous and others wondered if coming face-to-face with intense suffering could overwhelm Micah. But his parents, while acknowledging that the trip would not be an easy one, were convinced it was right because to do nothing in the face of injustice only leads to paralysis; it is not a healthy reaction to injustice. "I don't want him to despair," his father said. "What good is it to know of the suffering of others if we are not going to do anything about it? . . . To do nothing in response to genocide is to give up hope that we can uncover the Good and overcome evil."[14]

Micah's suitcase was lost en route to the Sudan, he was jet-lagged, and he experienced blistering heat of over a hundred degrees, but as he wrote in his travel journal, "I wasn't worried about going to a place where people live in garbage huts, but I have hope and joy that amounts to enough to fill up a whole planet." Chris bought hundreds of pounds of food, hired a truck and driver, and set off to the camp at Nyala, home of fourteen thousand "displaced persons" to whom he and Micah distributed the goods from the back of the truck. Micah was not prepared for the crowds who hounded the truck and pushed and shoved their way to the food, but he learned at firsthand a little about the extreme poverty and suffering in one corner of the world. He recorded in his travel journal, "The best part was asking a woman what her family ate today and having her say, 'It was amazing, these people came and brought rice, tomatoes, and onions and we all ate together.' . . . People say I went and saved people but I think differently. I might have contributed to the long hard period of work that needs to be done."

We offer our children our faith and the traditions of our religions. Jackson and Beckett, aged seven and three, are the

children of a Jewish mother and a Christian father, and their
parents have decided to raise the boys in both traditions. They
celebrate Passover and Easter, Christmas and Hanukkah. The
family has an Advent wreath and a Christmas tree and a
Hanukkah menorah. The children, or at least the eldest, who
is old enough to understand distinctions, are in no doubt as to
which parent is Jewish and which is Christian, nor about the
faith of their respective grandparents. The children may eventually decide to be either Jewish or Christian, but in the
meantime, they are growing up in the rich heritage of both
traditions.

We also help our children by resisting the commercialism
that invades our lives. Every day the mailbox is full of fliers,
catalogues, promotions, announcements of "bargain days,"
special offers. Ads dominate television and appear every time
the computer is turned on. Everywhere our children are
bombarded by the idea that happiness is to be found in buying—and the more we buy the happier we will be. For even
more happiness, there is eating—another bag of chips, another
burger, candy at the check-out counter, a doughnut from a
drive-by coffee shop, a snack at the gas station. How do we
steer children through the junk that they are presented with
every day of their lives?

Parents and caregivers have more power than they think.
They can offer children alternatives that truly satisfy so that
these become what children desire for themselves. Families
can hike, play in the city park, and take picnics on weekends.
Public libraries are free to all and there is no end to the books
and videos of all kinds that can be borrowed. There is not a
child I know who would rather sit in front of a video game
when a day swimming at the lake is offered. Museums are for
everybody—art, sculpture, and painting are there for children
as much as for adults. Science and technology museums fasci-
nate kids. And what child would pass up a chance to visit the
dinosaurs at a natural history museum? Or to explore the
planetarium or the aquarium or the zoo? Puppet shows
enthrall children; performances of *The Nutcracker* and *A*

Christmas Carol abound in winter, concerts and plays are available in the park all summer. No matter where we live, we can take our children by the hand and lead them into rich, nurturing experiences of culture, nature, and the arts.

As children mature, we can also encourage them to experience other places where life is very different from their home. Studying during their junior year in high school or college abroad, exploring an entirely new place or type of work during the "gap years" between finishing high school and beginning college, undertaking family service projects, building houses for Habitat for Humanity, volunteering in local soup kitchens and shelters for the homeless—these are all available for young people. Emily Dodge, the daughter of two well-paid bankers, spent a summer between her junior and senior years in high school participating in a service project in a small community in Honduras. She returned home and told her mother, "Time is better than money, and people are better than things. You don't need things to make you happy." Emily is now in college and hopes to become a lawyer working for human rights.

I interviewed Ramsay Hoke, a recent graduate of the University of North Carolina who decided to take a year off in Costa Rica working with youth and experiencing Latin America before beginning a job. "I learned the language in the street from the kids," he told me, "and worked at a community center as a tutor in geography, history, and math. Believe me," he continued,

> I learned a lot. There's not a lot of money in Costa Rica. The people don't have much materially—no cars, no luxuries—but they dress nicely. My friends were making $350 a month and they felt lucky to have jobs. Women are working in the factory for that and supporting four or five children at home. Family is much stronger with them than I had experienced here. And they also have a sense of place—"my town, my relatives"—these are important to them.

The experience has affected me. I see Americans alienated from everything—alienated from family, alienated from friends, alienated from themselves. In Costa Rica people are more content to relax, to take their time to solve their problems. They tolerate more and seem to have more fun. They love dancing. The party starts when it starts and never ends. Here everyone's too busy to take the time.

An experience like this can be hard and lonely. For the first three months I felt like I had no place and thought maybe I should go back to the States. I got robbed at gunpoint. It was tough, but I had two friends who were godsends. Every American needs to know what is going on in the rest of the world. I can't say enough about the experience, just the way it makes you think and feel differently. You can't gauge what's going on until you see the world in another context, from another perspective. It makes you wake up and realize the effect the U. S. has on other countries— politically, economically, socially.

When I interviewed Ramsay, he was back in Chapel Hill teaching English as a second language in the poorest neighborhood in the community.

The experience of living in other cultures at formative times in their lives will stay with our children and influence the course of their years. As parents and caregivers, as teachers and professors, as youth leaders, as godparents and grandparents we can show our children our rich world of art and culture, drama, music, and nature, and we can encourage them to see life from different perspectives. We teach our children best by example, by our just and loving lives. By taking action for justice, we demonstrate the meaning of prophetic hope. We teach our children zest for living by our own passion for life, the holiness of life by our own sense of the holy. We teach love by loving. We teach by our attitudes, by our affections, and by all the actions of our lives. A deep spirituality of everyday life cherishes our children, as we love, encourage, and nurture them. We become each other's teachers in the art of passion- ate engagement.

5

Opening the Doors
of Perception

*Make the universe your companion, always bearing in
mind the true nature of things. . . . For a person who has
the spirit, everything he sees becomes a flower, and
everything he imagines turns into the moon.*

—Bashō, *Learn from the Pine Tree*

Poetry and painting went together in the ancient Chinese
world. The painter would create the landscape on the silk
screen and then write a few words to express the mood and
spirit of the painting. The creation of paintings and poetry
were seen as spiritual exercises. Whatever the subject—
whether fish, rock, tree, or mountain—the artist, at the
moment of painting, was expected to *feel* its nature. If the subject was a tree, the artist felt the tree's strength shooting
through the branches and down into its roots; if a flower, the
artist felt the lightness and grace as its petals unfolded. When
painting a storm, the artist felt the rain and the crushing wind
as it tore trees from their roots and drenched the countryside.
One of the underlying principles of *bokugwa* (the name given
to this art form) was that the artist must experience the
essence of the subject and become one with it. To experience
the essence of the painting meant entering into the very heart

of its nature and becoming, as it were, the tree, the rock, the flower, the storm, the gently falling snow. The highest compliment to these artists was—and still is—to say that they painted from their soul and that their brushstrokes followed the dictates of their spirit.

Perhaps my most treasured painting is a watercolor done in Fontainbleau by my father when he was an art student between the two world wars. Discovered amidst family clutter long after our father's death, it pictures a stone bridge house and a graceful bridge over the river in Moret-sur-Loing. As children we knew almost nothing about our father's life as an artist except that he was talented and left France reluctantly to return home at the insistence of his mother, who persuaded him that he could not support himself as an artist. When we were young, Dad would sometimes get a faraway look in his eyes and tell us about his days of living and painting in France, but he never dwelt on it—nor, as far as we could determine, was he ever really contented after he left. But his painting of the stone bridge house was an epiphany for me and my brother Jay, and we set out one day from my home in Paris to see if we could find the location our father painted some sixty years earlier.

We descended from the train at Moret and asked how we could find the river. We had not walked far when Jay turned to me and exclaimed, "Look! That's it! That is it!" And sure enough, the tower was exactly as it was when my father had been there. As we drew closer we could see the detail of the cornices and even the lanterns on either side of the bridge were exactly as in the painting. The thrill of recognition quickened our pace. When we arrived we walked down to the river and paused, exactly where our father had stood. He was then twenty-one and very happy, living on the Left Bank in a community of artists and painting every day. We could feel that energy, that sense of his whole life lying before him, as we walked along the quay just as he had done on a beautiful day, warm and sunny. Jay opened up a picnic of a baguette, cheese, sausage, and a bottle of wine, and there we sat for what seemed like hours imagining our father the way he used to be.

Perhaps that is why my whole life has been enriched by artists who have opened up to me the beauty and the pain of the world. Our house is full of the works of artists, most of them unknown, some from the most desperate corners of the earth. I have brilliantly colored Haitian oil paintings depicting market workers—mostly women—carrying enormous baskets of fruit and vegetables on their heads and bearing bundles of sugarcane on their backs. Their immobile faces appear to mask the pain of their hard lives. On the home altar behind our wood stove there is a colorful Salvadoran nativity scene and a cross illustrating images of village life. They are cheerful and bright. Beside them is a painting on glass of Jesus' triumphal entry into Jerusalem. This "icon"—as the artist calls it—was the gift a fourteen-year-old boy who is one of the thousands of children living in the tunnels and on the streets of Bucharest.

We have a colored pencil drawing of a family gathered around a dining table held by God's hands. Underneath, written in Albanian, are the words, "God holds the family in his loving hands and keeps us firmly in his palms." Nikkola Hanxhari, another fourteen-year-old, gave me this drawing when I visited the home of his parents in Tirana. His sister, Kristina, jokes that Nikkola just can't stop drawing, that he would draw every waking moment if he could. A hand-built ceramic plaque of the Holy Family was created by a sculptor who lives in the l'Arche community for the mentally challenged in Trosly-Breuil in France, a gift given to us by its founder, Jean Vanier, when we visited. Two malachite eggs, one green and the other pink, were made by a Dutch friend; they sit beside another very different egg from Russia, which portrays a stylized Virgin Mary with a glossy finish.

One of my favorite works of art is a "story cloth" made by a Hmong woman in a Thai refugee camp while waiting for asylum in the United States. In colorful fine thread she has illustrated the journey of the Hmong people. The first scene has a man and woman sitting at a campfire outside their simple home in the mountains of Laos, where trees and plants and a small vegetable garden growing beside the dwelling suggest a peaceful life. Moving across the cloth are planes flying over, then planes dropping bombs and homes erupting into flames. Further down the story cloth Hmong families are pictured, their backs heavy with possessions, as they walk toward the Mekong River to be floated across in inner tubes and on simple bamboo rafts. They are finally welcomed by officials at the refugee camp just over the border from Laos. These Thai story cloths are the only artistic representations of the Vietnam War.

Some of my favorite pieces are woodcut prints from Japan, gifts to us from our son in Kyoto. Japanese woodcut printing originated in ancient China and was brought to Japan with the introduction of Buddhism. Two of Japan's greatest woodcut artists of the eighteenth century are Hiroshiga and Hokusai, and we are privileged to have views of Mount Fuji by each of them. Hokusai's Fuji picture has cranes in the foreground while Hiroshiga's has chrysanthemums, both Japanese symbols of long life. Another woodcut, this one from South America, is completely different—a wide sweeping view of the sun setting over the Rio de la Plata at Punta del Este in Uruguay. It is by Uruguay's most renowned living artist, Carlos Paez Vilero, who just happened to be in his studio when we stopped by and signed the print for us. It recalls a happy day we spent visiting an island off Punta del Este, and it makes me smile because a freighter in the foreground of the print bears the "Tri-colour," the French national flag.

What is the significance to me personally of these works of art that fill our house and surround our life? Most of these works were gifts, so they all tell a story or evoke the memory of a person or a part of the world that is special to us. Every time I look at the Salvadoran and Haitian works, I marvel at the vitality of the people whose countries they represent who have been so cruelly oppressed and tortured. To me they are works of resurrection, symbols of a faith that will not be killed by oppressors. The "Triumphal Entry into Jerusalem" icon was given to me following a day of interviewing young people who live on the streets of Bucharest for a magazine article. One of my hosts from the Orthodox Church in Romania, Rodica, regularly visits with the children and brings baskets of food. One afternoon I went with her to a subway station not far from her office. Almost immediately about a dozen boys and girls emerged from the tunnels to greet her and receive her gifts. These children had been abandoned by their families during the years when Romania's dictator, Nicolae Ceausescu, ruled that Romanian parents should have at least six children to build up the country's labor force. Although parents loved their children they could not care for so many; thus thousands of children ended up in the streets and in orphanages. I asked the group gathered around Rodica, "Who is your family?" One twelve-year-old, putting his arm around his companions, said, "Here is my family." This little family of the subway tunnels gives me hope.

In a commentary for an art exhibition of children's art in wartime, Robert Coles, author of the series *Children of Crisis,* had this to say: "A drawing or a painting is a soul's message eagerly sought by us watchful onlookers. Whether the artist be grown up or a boy or girl, the point is to demonstrate what has been imagined or, yes, witnessed."[15] He points out that these boys and girls become our teachers through their works of art, broadening our perspective and our ability to respond in our minds and hearts. These young people who live in the streets and in tunnels under Bucharest taught me something similar about sheer courage and endurance and the remarkable resilience of the human spirit. When I look at the icon painted by the Romanian street child, courage and hope is the message it carries to my soul.

▪　　▪　　▪

What works of art adorn your walls and your life? What roots of your being do they tap into? Who are your favorite artists? Why do you prefer some to others? What sorts of art speak to your soul? What does art have to do with a spirituality of everyday life? How does art enhance your own spiritual life? How does art build up the commonwealth of God? Where is God encountered through works of art? Simply contemplating one or two of these questions will begin to open up for you the doors to perception. The artist sees the world with a heightened sensitivity, and urges us to do so as well. Art brings us close to the heart of the world, created and cherished by the Holy God of creation, and the artist creates from the raw elements of the universe just as God created the world.

Vincent Van Gogh is easily my favorite artist. I have been to his cornfields and seen his gypsy camps, walked in his footsteps along the Rhone and strolled in the Alpilles outside of Arles where he attempted to establish an artists' community. I have also visited Auvers where he painted the crooked church and later ended his life. I warm to his passion and his love of color, I experience his emotions and the fervor of his faith. I also see his sadness and sense of desolation, sense his descent into madness. Many of Van Gogh's early paintings are somber and dark, like the *Potato Eaters,* but when he found his stride he reveled in texture and colors in their vast array. He absorbed the energy of the Provençal cornfields he painted and the character of his subjects. Van Gogh's *Starry Night,* painted on the side of the Rhone River during his two years in Arles, illustrates this heightened consciousness. As Van Gogh wrote to his brother:

> *Starry Night* was painted during the night by the light under a gas lamp. The sky is blue-green, the water royal blue, the land mauve. The town is blue and violet, the gaslight yellow with reddish reflections going down to bronze-green. On the blue-green sky the Great Bear twinkles green and rises in the paleness which contrasts with the brutal gold of the gaslight.[16]

By immersing himself in his painting, Van Gogh invites the viewer to experience it with him. In Arles I have stood at the bend in the Rhone where Van Gogh painted *Starry Night,* and

I feel some of the intensity that went into the painting. I delight in the stars and the city lights shimmering on the river. If it is a warm evening my wanderings may take me up to the café he painted, now called Café of the Evening. I will sit outside under the stars and enjoy a cup of coffee while thinking about what Van Gogh himself said of this painting:

> This café at night is a new painting showing the outside of a café in the evening. On the terrace appear small figures of people drinking. An enormous yellow lantern illuminates the terrace, the outside wall and the pavement, and even projects on to the cobbles of the street which take on a tint of violet-rose. The gables of the houses in a side street, extending under a blue night sky filled with stars, are painted dark blue, and there is a green tree.[17]

How else can art bring us closer to the heart of the world? It can nurture the feelings of connectedness. Being at Moret-sur-Loing gave me an appreciation of my father years after his death. In my mind's eye I now picture him smiling and happy, not the ill, burdened, depressed man he was to become, a failure in his own eyes. His paintings are a healing presence in my life.

The artist also gives us a glimpse of heaven. Unquestionably religion has been the world's greatest inspiration for the creation of artistic works. From their devotion, artists have created every kind of expression of faith, from the mosaics of the great Byzantine cathedrals to the frescos of gothic Europe and from the temple art of the East to the decoration of chapels, stupas, temples, cathedrals, mosques, and wayside shrines. So we might ask the question: Must the subject matter of a particular work need to be religious for the art to be considered religious? Does it have to be the Sistine Chapel ceiling or Fra Angelico's *Annunciation* to be considered religious? Marc Chagall, who worked with both religious and secular themes, would not say so. His paintings of scenes from the Hebrew scriptures displayed in the Chagall Museum in Nice evoke the

same sense of deep wonder as his whimsical paintings of the
townspeople suspended in the air over his home in Vitebsk.
Nor did Chagall make any distinction between art, life, and
religion, saying, "There are hundreds of moments in life
which are linked together by art, and turn into paintings. . . . [Paintings] are a continuation of life."[18] Van Gogh,
also deeply religious, rarely painted religious subjects. Once
when painting an infant he said, "I think I see something
deeper, more infinite, more eternal than the ocean in the
expression of the eyes of a little baby when it wakes in the
morning, and coos or laughs when it sees the sun shining on
its cradle. If there is a 'ray on high' perhaps one can find it
there."[19] Evidently theologian Paul Tillich would agree, for he
said, "When we look at pictures by Van Gogh we experience
the power of being." Art makes us aware, he wrote, of something completely new.[20]

Creating the universe was God's first activity, and through
their works artists carry us just a little closer to the creativity
of God. Artists touch the creative impulse in us all and remind
us that as children we were all artists. Children see before they
speak and write. Children draw, coloring the blue sky above,
the sun's rays. They color the earth, usually in a luminous
green, and they cover it with brightly drawn flowers. They
draw what they see and love—parents, brothers and sisters,
family pets.

■   ■   ■

As adults the arts enhance our lives in many ways, and two in
particular. First, when we open our eyes to see the world
through the images presented to us by the artist, we can learn
to magnify our feeling for the beauty all around us, to quicken
our consciences, to connect us to individuals we know and
love and those whose brave lives we admire, such as those
who suffer in Haiti and El Salvador. Art opens up channels
within and quickens our sense of empathy. Art delights and

opens the heart. Art brings us close to the supreme artist of the universe, to God.

Harry Jackson, whose sculptures and paintings are on display in his studio in Cody, Wyoming, as well as in museums and galleries around the world, once told me, "Every aspect of art is a reflection of the Divine Presence. The artist is a medium, a vessel, a channel, for the greater power. Without question. Without question. The artist is, in some small way, the vehicle through which the Divine is revealed."

▪ ▪ ▪

Second, the arts give us the chance to awaken the artist within by taking up a sketch pad and just starting to draw. This is not a matter of *talent,* it is a matter of *desire,* the desire to be closer to the heart of creation by letting its beauty flow through the eye and into hand or brush. In his book on drawing, the Dutch artist and writer Frederick Franck answers the question "Who is the artist?" by saying the artist "is the unspoiled core of everyone before he is choked by schooling, training, conditioning until the artist shrivels up and is forgotten." Franck believes, however, that "the core is never killed completely. At times it responds to nature, to beauty, to life, suddenly aware again of being in the presence of a mystery that baffles understanding and which only has to be glimpsed to renew our spirit and to make us feel that life is a supreme gift."

I picked up a copy of Franck's book as I was driving through Lawrence, Kansas, and happened upon the public library's annual secondhand book sale. I must have been ready for this book because even though I was tired at the end of the day, I read the book from cover to cover in the motel room that night. Franck expressed what I intuitively had known was the case: "The eye is the lens of the heart, open to the world."[21]

Since Franck invites one to just take up a brush and draw from the soul, I thought I would try it. We were staying in a *kayabuki,* a traditional thatched-roof farmhouse in the tiny hamlet of Hattoji, tucked high up in the mountains of western Japan. The house overlooked lush, terraced rice fields on three sides. The view from the fourth side carried the eye through a thick grove of bamboo trees up to the mountain peak. The only audible sounds were the croaking of frogs from the wet rice paddies, bird songs, and in the evening the insistent droning of cicadas. Yes, here was the place to try my hand at drawing, something I had not done since high school and for which I never had any particular talent. I felt like a fool—what was this usually sensible person doing? Nonetheless, I took up a pad and pencil, and I started with the rice field in front of the house. As I sat before the field, I noticed the individual leaves of the rice plants, paper thin but erect, their points bending slightly at their tops. I absorbed their iridescent green color and focused on just one or two of the leaves. Then I started to draw, and as I did so I felt the beauty of the plants overpower me and, yes, even a feeling of being somehow in tune with the plants.

The next day I took my pencil and pad into the bamboo grove. Here it was cool and fragrant. I began by enjoying coolness, and then my mind turned to the beauty of the trees. They were large and small, thick and slender; their trunks all carried horizontal lines as regular intervals. They stood straight and tall. A few grew at an angle, but I observed that bamboo trunks do not bend and sway like the trees in my part of the world, nor were there other varieties of trees and plants present in the grove. It was just bamboo, and lots of it. Then I began to draw just what I was seeing and feeling. Immersed in such lovely trees, I lost myself; I forgot all about time. I felt a deep sense of peace. Outside the grove the temperature was close to ninety on a hot August afternoon, but after finishing the drawing and coming out into the sun, I felt just as refreshed as if I had taken a swim in a cool mountain pool.

■   ■   ■

The poet and the painter are partners in perception, along with the musician and the writer of prose, the photographer and the quilter, the woodworker, the potter, and the gardener. They touch the heartbeat of God's world and invite us to do the same. We all have the opportunity to become artisans in our extravagantly beautiful world created and beloved by God. As Bashō, Japan's most famous poet, suggests, we can make the "universe our companion" through immersion in the arts, both through appreciation and participation. Through the arts we can open our doors of perception and find passionate engagement with the world's suffering and anguish, its beauty and joy.

6

Loving the Earth and Keeping the Garden

Love all creation, the whole of it and every grain of sand.
Love every leaf, every ray of God's light. Love the ani-
mals, love the plants, love everything. If you love every-
thing, you will perceive the divine mystery of things.
— Fyodor Dostoyevsky, *The Brothers Karamazov*

Have you ever lain on a newly mown field on a sunny summer afternoon, inhaling the damp, pungent aroma of the hay,
listening to the birds and crickets, and felt for a fleeting
moment—for just an instant—that you *were* the hay, that you
were its sweet smell, that you were at one with the earth
beneath you? Or lay awake at night listening to the ocean?
Once I was staying in a guest house high above a section of
rocky crevices on the shore of the Mediterranean. The waves
would come crashing in, carrying the pebbles with them and
then dragging them out again. The rhythm reverberated up to
my tiny room, in and out all night long, a rhythm as old as the
dawn of the earth and as new as tonight. Listening to the
waves' regular motion in the still of the night, I noticed that
my heart beat to their rhythm and even my breathing kept
their pace, in and out, in and out, until they carried me off to
sleep, rocked into calmness by the motion. I rested in the deep

sense of being at one with the waves and with the rhythmic, creative force of the universe.

Fortunately, reminders of our oneness with the creation lurk even in the most unsuspected places, where the natural world even in its most pristine state seems to be in dire straits. The Shawangunk Mountains are a small range of old mountains wedged between the Alleghenies and the Catskills in New York state, with thousands of acres of lush, untouched scenery and massive rock formations. A unique feature is that stone-edged mountain lakes are to be found on the mountaintops; they are surrounded by boulders that plunge into deep waters below. Last year we walked around Lake Minnewaska, admiring the lake and the views over upland meadows and farms and to the mountains beyond. Just an hour and a half north of New York City, we could by all appearances have been in northern Ontario. But we were dismayed to learn that, in fact, the lake is dead due to acid rain. It is full of mercury and void of all the life one expects of mountain lakes, like turtles and trout and frogs.

We are the most creative species that has ever inhabited the earth as well as the most destructive; only human beings have within themselves the capacity and the power to destroy the Creator's creation. It is only now that our lakes are dead, our seas polluted, our ancient forests cut down, and our earth denuded of minerals that we shrink back in horror at what our species has done to this planet. The fatal flaw that Christians throughout the ages have employed to justify their rape of the land is part of the Creation story, where God gives humans dominion over the species of the earth along with the command to "till the earth and subdue it." It is only now that we realize just what poor stewards we have been. It is only now, with the stores of oil under the earth and sea depleted, that we realize the devastation petroleum has caused on this earth— contaminated air, despoiled coastlines, poisoned international relations, the rationale for war upon war. We are like the drug addict who functions with his daily fix but knows in his heart that the habit is slowly killing him. The developed world is hooked; its economy and way of life are built and maintained by an everflowing supply of oil. What is required to save our precious environment is a complete turning around, something on the order of a religious conversion to Planet Earth. Helen Caldicott, cofounder of Physicians for Social Responsibility, posed the question, "Can we evolve spiritually and emotionally in time to control the overwhelming evil that our advanced and rational intellect has created?"[22]

As lovers of life and all that is good and true and authentic, we will unflinchingly answer, "Yes, we can. We will evolve spiritually and emotionally in order to save our precious creation." But we will only protect what we deeply love and cherish. The question then becomes *how*. How do we cherish the earth?

In seeking an answer, we might regard the earth as we do our aging, perhaps frail but still beautiful mothers. Just as we will do anything to help, comfort, and protect our mothers, so we must do the same for our Mother Earth. If we have not done so already, the first thing to do in developing a planetary spiritually is to fall in love, or fall in love again, with God's beautiful earth. As St. Basil the Great wrote centuries ago, "I want creation to penetrate you with so much admiration that everywhere you may be, the least plant may bring you the clear remembrance of the Creator."

There are a million recipes for falling in love with the earth, depending upon who you are and how you look at the world. I can only tell you how I rekindle my love affair with the earth. I drive across the high plains of Kansas near Council Grove. The shadows are deepening as the sun reddens the western sky. Silhouetted are a few clumps of high blue stem grass, a lonely tree, but otherwise just the gently undulating prairie stretching to the far reaches of the horizon. Or back home in Connecticut I drive along the road beside the Connecticut River in the early evening. I pull over for a moment to pause while the descending sun paints a shimmering red carpet across the flat water. It is as if all creation were stopped just for a minute or two to praise the Creator who made this lovely tableau.

I am blessed by living in a part of the country where there are all kinds of nature preserves and state parks. Every afternoon when I am home, except in the summer, I take a walk on one of hundreds of trails. I know most of them well, and I look forward to the brook that I am coming to just around the next bend, to the fresh skunk cabbage in the spring and the sea of mountain laurel that blooms in May. In the fall I observe whether the squirrels are furiously gathering acorns, and if so I know that a cold and snowy winter lies ahead. And when winter comes the path is icy, but the air is cool and refreshing. The bare trees against the snow have a stark beauty to them, and there are places where the white and dark of winter are punctuated with winterberry bushes splendid in their scarlet clumps of berries.

But summers are too hot for me, so I swim. I swim in all conditions—in the brilliant burning sun on hundred-degree afternoons, in the rain, in storms, and when the pond is a perfectly still reflecting mirror. I have discovered a lonely pond in the woods not far from my house. It is a little hike to get there but the pond is as pristine as the day it was first created, so my walk to it is rewarded. No dwelling hugs its shore and only once or twice in a summer will I have a fisherman for company. But every day I have turtles, frogs, fish nipping lightly at my legs, a pair of hawks circling overhead. On rare occasions a stately blue heron stands erect at the end of the pond. My presence does not frighten her off. As I swim the length of the pond, the cool water refreshes my body and revives my soul. I glide through a patch of lilies and I look down through the perfectly clear water, and I marvel at the artistry of the Creator who made "my secret pond." A green bullfrog hears my approach and dives off a rock. I play a game with the turtles—from afar I can see them sunning themselves on a half-submerged tree trunk and I try to approach them noiselessly, so quietly that I do not disturb them. If I swim by without unsettling them, I win. But usually they are smarter than I am, and I hear their hollow plop as they dive into the water.

It was mid–September last year and the water, after a week of brisk evenings, was becoming too cold to swim in comfortably. I realized that the day's swim would be my last for the season. To my delight, a pair of Canada geese were at the pond when I arrived. When they noticed me they honked and continued to do so as they followed me down to the end of the pond and back. I marveled at their smooth passage through the still water, their gracefully held heads. I felt for just a moment at one with my two sleek and elegant companions. Soon I would leave the pond for the afternoon and for the season, carrying with me the memory of feeling absolutely in tune with my body, with the fresh pond water and all its hidden aquatic life, the rocks and trees at the edge and the blue sky above. This would be a memory to savor through the dark, gray days of winter and cause to give profound thanks to our Creator God of the universe.

■   ■   ■

But one does not have to live in the country to fall in love with God's precious creation. Living in the city is no barrier to developing an appreciation of the natural world. When I lived in Paris I developed an appreciation of city birds and their resiliency. I remember one early spring morning standing a long time on Pont Marie observing just one pigeon. Its claws were gnarled and crooked, no doubt from many hard landings on the city's rock and concrete, yet this ordinary pigeon stiffened its body, posed for takeoff, and glided away beautifully and noiselessly into the Paris smog. This one bird got me thinking about the resiliency of pigeons.

My friends Joyce and Ray discovered a family of pigeons living on the dark, almost forgotten balcony of their Munich apartment just outside their kitchen window. First Joyce noticed one of the birds flying toward the balcony with sticks in her mouth, and she began to observe the same flights every day. There was a lull in activity and Joyce and Ray forgot about the pigeons until one afternoon when their eyes fell upon the terrace and they beheld a family of six young pigeons. Now their interest had been piqued, and they ate their breakfast every morning entranced with the growth and development of the pigeon family. First the adult pigeons would bring food for their young; then gradually they guided them out of the nest to take their first flights. By midsummer the family had left the nest completely, leaving Ray and Joyce hoping that they would return again in the late winter and renew their cycle of creativity.

Pigeons represent the extent to which living beings can adapt to crowded, unpropitious environments and still thrive. They have occupied urban spaces from time immemorial and have developed all the necessary coping skills. I think people are the same way. They will find a piece of the natural world in the city, and they will flourish even when the circumstances are most adverse, just like the people of the Island View neighborhood of Detroit. This 123-block area once held the gracious residences of Detroit's elite, who long since had departed for the suburbs. The formerly grand mansions, burned down and demolished, became a wasteland of some thousand empty lots. But only for a while. Detroit's urban desert now blooms as lot after lot has been taken over and converted into a garden. Rocks and debris have given way to tomatoes, strawberries, corn, lettuce, and all manner of squash. Flowers bloom everywhere. The lots prosper due to the loving attention of neighbors, old and young, who have fallen in love with the garden and keep it with pride and pleasure. When I lived in New York City I would stretch out on the grass in the Barnard College Yard across the street from where I lived. In Paris I would do the same on a sunny afternoon at Place des Vosges, or I would ride my bicycle along the Seine and let its lapping waters wash away the stress of the day. City dwellers tend window boxes, they grow rooftop and empty lot gardens; they fill their southern exposure windows with flowers and plants. As they do so they touch the creativity of the Creator God of the universe.

The great Persian poet Rumi tells us that "there is a community of the spirit. Join in, and feel the delight of walking in the noisy street, and *being* the noise."[23] This is why city parks were invented, and this is why they are cherished. They are natural places amidst the towers of urban life where one breathes just a little more easily and feels real grass underfoot. Rivers and canals running through cities also connect us with the flow of life. Even a clump of grass forcing its tender blades through cracked city sidewalks is a reminder that the natural world is not far from us. I think people, all people, have an urge to connect with living, growing nature. For those who are truly awake to the awesome mystery of God's creation, everything in the natural world is a reminder of the gracious God of the universe whose presence we feel in every gust of wind or shower of rain.

After we fall in love with God's precious creation, it hurts us to see it harmed. The ugly scars on a tree-stripped mountainside give us pain. Earthmovers cutting through the lovely Sunshine Valley in a hidden corner of Montana to build a new road jar our sensibilities. Dead lakes, oil-slicked coastlines, schools of fish lying belly-up, poisoned air, trees browning in spring when they should be greening—all remind us that our earth is wounded. A Coloradoan poet and woodcarver, Robert O'Rourke, told me about a ride through the Chuska Mountains on a rough, rugged road close to Canyon de Chelly. All along the route trees were bulldozed, rocks dynamited, and the earth broken and scarred. "It seemed to me," he said, "that even the rocks cried out in pain."

■   ■   ▩

There are all kinds of ways to rekindle our love affair with the earth, no matter where we live or where we find ourselves on a given day. Take a moment, any time, any place, even walking down a crowded city street, and pause. Stand quietly and look up. Notice the sunset lighting up the western sky. Look at the brilliant oranges and reds moving across the sky lighting the heavens, and then as the light recedes, watch darkness begin its descent over the land. Or, at the dawn of the day, sit and watch the rising golden sun dispel the shadows and wake the city for another day. Feel the seasons. In the Northern Hemisphere, feel the first chill of autumn in late August. Listen for the honking of Canada geese flying over your dwelling. Wait for the yellowing and reddening of the maple trees, the first snow, the soil under your feet in mid-winter, hard as iron, the frost-scattered patterns on the window pane, the Christmas blizzard. Feel the power of the roaring wind as it scatters a carpet of snow over the dark city. When the wind subsides, listen to the hush, the gentle quietness of snow lightly falling. Finally, when the snow has stopped and the sun has returned, revel in the beauty of the white world all around you under the cloudless, cerulean sky.

As March nears, look for the first signs of spring—the soil softening underfoot, releasing its grip on winter; the willows beginning to put on their yellow coats, crocuses and daffodils starting to shoot up their green leaves after their long winter's nap, buds appearing on the elm trees, grass slowly greening. Watch for the day, coming soon, when there is an explosion of brilliant, iridescent green everywhere, from each blade of new grass to the new tender leaves of the trees that grow even in the middle of Broadway in New York City. Watch for the return of the robins.

Savor the summer. Walk the beach and feel the soft sand between your toes. Dive into the waves and ride them to the shore. Feel the refreshing water encircle your body. Feel the power of the sea as the undertow tries to pull you out. Let your eye follow the busy sandpipers as they industriously hasten along the water's edge, and marvel at the beauty of the gulls circling above, just waiting for you to toss them a crumb from your sandwich. Lie back in the supple sand and feel the sun warming you through to your core. The beach is the Sabbath of God's creation, its clock is the flow of the tide, where, on any day at all, you can feel its rhythms and become engulfed in its splendor.

God continues the work of creating, sustaining, and protecting the earth through us, doing our part in tending the garden. Passionate engagement in our day includes our listening to the song of the earth, falling passionately in love with it, defending and protecting our sacred land so that it and our descendants may live and flourish.

7

The Eleventh Commandment: Hospitality

We exist for each other, and when we're at a low ebb, sometimes just to see the goodness radiating from another can be all we need in order to rediscover ourselves.

—Kathleen Norris, *The Cloister Walk*

It was a Sunday evening after a busy day. We had finished dinner and were getting ready to put our three small children to bed. My husband Jeffery was serving as a summer minister to two small Vermont congregations, and he was tired after church services and an afternoon full of parish meetings. We were looking forward to a quiet evening. Then the phone rang. The caller asked to speak with the pastor, and before I knew it Jeffery was walking to the car to drive to the bus station across the river to pick up the man who only told him that he needed a place to stay for the night. He did not listen to my protests: "What do you know about this guy? How can we have a stranger stay with us about whom we know absolutely nothing? It's not safe. Think of the children. We were just getting ready to relax and read the Sunday paper." Jeffery brushed away my worries, telling me to relax as he tried to assure me that everything would be all right.

Twenty minutes later Jeffery returned with John, a middle-aged, ragged man with worn clothes carrying a small pack. He told us neither where he had come from nor where he was headed. All we knew was that he seemed pleased to be with us. We invited him to sit in the living room while I prepared him a meal. He did not say much; he seemed tired and pleased to relax into a soft chair. He had a certain presence about him that was captivating to the children, who sat in rapt attention at his feet. When I gave him his dinner he ate it with relish and then licked the plate. Chris at age six commented, "You must have been *very* hungry." He acknowledged that indeed he was but that he was feeling better now. He moved to sit on the floor with the children and told them he had a surprise for them. John opened his pack and removed about a dozen Indian brass bells in varying sizes. They were small, engraved with floral patterns, and beautiful. John rang them all and invited the children to do the same.

He had in just an hour or so built up a bond with the children and it was only with reluctance that I finally got them off to bed. John, Jeffery, and I soon followed. We offered John a bed in a downstairs room, while we went to our room upstairs in the small Cape Cod–style house that was our summer home. All the family fell quickly asleep, but Jeffery and I were awakened a little later by a voice that carried up the stairs. We strained our ears. It was John talking. But what was he saying? My nervousness at having a stranger under our roof returned, and I pushed Jeffery out of bed to go downstairs to inspect. Quietly he descended the stairs and did not return for ten or so minutes. As the minutes passed so my disease mounted. He returned shamefaced, reporting that as he listened outside John's closed door he heard our guest praying by name for each member of the family—deep, heartfelt, and insightful prayers.

In the morning John played with the children while I cooked breakfast, then returned to the bus station and passed out of our lives. Or did he? Of one thing we were all clear: our family had had an angel in our midst, just like the passage from the letter to the Hebrews, "Do not neglect to show hospitality to strangers, for by doing so some have entertained angels unawares" (13:2). Humbled and chagrined though I was, John had taught me a lesson in hospitality.

Many years later my son Chris, who had been so enthralled with John's bells, received hospitality half a world away in the mountains of Japan after he and a friend became lost on a hike in Kyoto's Higashiyama Mountains. They left in the middle of the afternoon and the first part of the hike went through temple gardens, past a shrine, and entered thick woods. They were captivated by the beauty of the fall colors, the late afternoon sun on the brilliant reds and yellows of the maples, but the euphoria did not last as they entered the darkening forest and felt less and less sure of the way. Before long the light had faded and they knew they were lost, furiously working their way along the ridge, climbing one small peak after another, exhausted and drenched with sweat. Finally emerging from the woods beside a narrow mountain road, they saw the lights of a small traditional wooden building. Out rushed a small Japanese woman of about sixty, saying, "Welcome, welcome! Please come in. I bet you boys could use a hot bath." They could not believe their luck—they had come out of the woods directly alongside a traditional Japanese hot spring bath.

"Despite the fact that it was nearly closing time, the woman ushered us into the waiting room of the bath and told us to make ourselves comfortable. This we were more than happy to do, since we were just about dead on our feet," Chris reported later when he told us his story. "There was a kerosene heater in the room, and the woman soon came bustling out of the office with a pot of hot tea. It was absolute nectar, and we drank it as fast as its temperature would allow.

"After drinking tea for a while the woman asked us if we were ready for the bath. We nodded in assent and the woman gave us each a towel and led us to the changing room. We peeled off our soaking clothes and entered the bathing area. The bath was extremely simple—just one big tub steaming in the middle of a tiled room. We splashed buckets of water over ourselves from the tub to clean off the dirt and sweat, and then we plunged into the tub. It was paradise! At that moment, no amount of money could have bought a more perfect or welcome pleasure.

"Just as we were preparing to leave, the woman emerged from her office and collared the Japanese man who had joined us in the bath. After a brief discussion in Japanese, she announced to us that she had convinced the man to drive us back to our bikes. We were just about speechless with gratitude, since neither of us much fancied the idea of a long walk in wet clothes along a dark mountain road. As we left the hot spring, the woman gave each of us a bottle of water from the spring that fed the bath, which she said had healing qualities. We then piled into the man's car and he set off down the hill toward Kyoto. The man seemed a little nervous to have two foreigners in his car, but soon he relaxed and we had a good chat. When he dropped us beside our bikes at the trailhead, we both stood there shaking our heads. Was our adventure in the woods and that fantastic hot spring bath merely a figment of our tired imaginations? It seemed like that was indeed the case, but each of us was carrying a bottle of delicious spring water. For the next week, each time we had a sip of it, it reminded us of the kindness we had received up on the mountain."

▪ ▪ ▪

Hospitality is a universal human virtue, and it was one of the defining marks of early Christian communities. Whatever they had they readily shared with the poor, the widows, and the orphans. Christians were hospitable to travelers and welcomed strangers into their homes. I have no doubt that one of the reasons Christianity spread so quickly was their habit of hospitality. About 140 CE the Greek philosopher Aristides sent a letter to Emperor Antonius Pius describing what he observed of Christian hospitality:

They walk in all humility and kindness.... They love one another. From the widows they do not turn their countenance and they rescue the orphan. He who has gives to him who has not without grudging, and when they see the stranger they bring him to their dwellings and rejoice over him as over a true brother.[24]

As Christianity spread and became more organized, Christian communities established hospitals, hostels, hospices, and houses of hospitality. Monastic communities received guests, just as they continue to do today. The special intention was the welcome of the stranger, the vulnerable, the weak and sick, the alien—those who lived on the fringes who lacked the help, care, and protection of friends and family. Hospitality was to be extended without any expectation of return or payment.

The biblical understanding of hospitality extends far deeper than what we have come in our day to regard as hospitality, the entertaining of friends and family and business associates. Biblical hospitality involves a mutual giving and receiving, a mutual respect between guest and host, a sharing not only of food and drink but of compassion for the other and the joy of being in the company of another precious child of God. It often involves the crossing of social divisions, barriers of class, culture, nationality, and race. In a sense, God is the host and God is the guest who comes into our home, as John did so many years ago. Christine Pohl, who has written the beautiful and definitive book on the recovery of hospitality in our age, *Making Room,* holds:

> The distinctive Christian contribution was the emphasis on including the poor and neediest, the ones who could not return the favor. This focus did not diminish the value of hospitality to family and friends; rather, it broadened the practice so that the close relations formed by table fellowship and conversation could be extended to the most vulnerable.[25]

Hospitality in our age has become so institutionalized that we tend to forget its ancient roots as a natural extension and fruit of the belief that we meet Christ in neighbor and stranger alike, and that like Christ we are to provide for the needs of others. But the provision of hospitality is probably a more basic human endeavor that transcends religion and culture. The world is full of people who reach out to others, such as the compassionate woman at the mountain bath house who took in my son. The institutionalization of hospitality has been positive in that towns and cities provide rooms for the homeless, and churches sponsor soup kitchens and food pantries. Community shelters offer refuge for victims of abuse or persecution or natural disaster. Hospices for the dying have also been established, and it is the law that anyone, regardless of ability to pay, has to be received and treated in hospital emergency rooms. The profession of social work arose to offer social assistance for individuals and families in a variety of situations. Most schools have social workers now, and many also have breakfast programs in areas where children often have to leave home in the morning without eating any food. Most of these institutional programs of hospitality are taken for granted, and rightly so, but it is also fair to say that sometimes institutional service lacks a human touch and that no amount of community hospitality can take the place of individuals, families, and household groups offering hospitality.

■　▓　▓

Hospitality takes many forms, three in particular: the hospitality of the home and hearth, the hospitality of the highways and byways, and the hospitality of the heart.

I learned about the hospitality of the home and hearth on one of those rainy, bone-chilling days in New Haven in February, going door-to-door carrying out a survey of houses and apartments that had received federal government grants to improve housing in depressed urban areas. It was about two in the afternoon, I was tired and hungry, and no one responded to my knocks on the door of the four-story walk-up with the metal stairs on the exterior of the building. As I was descending the stairs, however, the door on the second floor opened. The elderly Italian woman inside told me she noticed me pass by her kitchen and that I looked cold and tired. Would I like to come in and warm up?

She ushered me into a steaming kitchen where a huge pan of tomato sauce boiled on an old black iron range. On the table stood a bowl of eggplant and four long, fragrant loaves of crusty bread that had just come from the oven. Asking no questions, she just sat me down and poured a glass of wine. She cut into one of the loaves, covered it with eggplant, and poured sauce over it. I never learned her name, but I can truthfully say that I have had no finer Italian dinner anyplace, ever.

This is how we most commonly think of hospitality, and it is also the most risky because it takes the stranger or visitor right into the heart of our personal and geographic space. The door is opened, the curtain parted, the veil is lifted, and the stranger comes into our life for a while. We are not talking about social engagements like dinner parties or opportunities to show off our newest recipes, although these might be included, but about allowing a guest to come into our lives by opening up a channel to give and receive life and nurture from the other. Unless we give freely of ourselves, it is not authentic hospitality. An occasion used for social or business advantage is not true hospitality; a business lunch is just that, a business lunch. An authentic hospitality of the home and hearth forms and nurtures; it is life-giving, and can even change your life. The ancient Rule of St. Benedict, dating from the sixth century, puts a premium on the role of hospitality: "All guests who present themselves are to be welcomed as Christ, for he himself said, 'I was a stranger and you welcomed me' (Matt. 25:35)."[26]

I owe my faith to a Lakota woman who took me into her home and life when I was a naïve nineteen-year-old at a summer church work camp in Okreek, a minuscule hamlet along

Highway 18 on the Rosebud Indian Reservation in South Dakota. If you blink driving by, you'll miss it. I had no high and lofty purpose in participating—it took me away from the summer waitressing and babysitting jobs and endless nightly beer parties that were the usual fare of college students in my hometown. When I filled out the application to go to the Rosebud for the summer I made up some respectable reason as a cover, so imagine my surprise when I "got religion" through the hospitality of Nancy Lambert.

Our little group consisted of about ten students. Girls lived in the Guild Hall, a freestanding church hall, and the guys in a tent outside. Plumbing was a two-seater out in the back, and our water came from the town pump outside our kitchen door. If we wanted to make a phone call we had to go up to the town's only phone at the gas station on Highway 18. Once a week the principal of the town school invited us to his house for a shower. The rest of the days we bathed in the stock pond a short walk over the bluff. During the days everyone except for me was occupied with building the foundation for the local church, while I went into Mission a few miles down Highway 18 to help the minister's wife run her Girl Scout summer program.

After supper all the work camp members would go out to the empty lot and play softball, but to avoid humiliation I stayed well away from the game. Instead, I would go across to Granny Lambert's house, just beyond the town pump, and sit on her front step for hours, sometimes listening to her stories and other times just sitting in silence as the evening sneaked in and covered the land. Sometimes she offered me a snack or a cup of coffee, but for the most part her hospitality was solely her presence and her transparency. Members of her extended family treated me as one of them. One of my favorite of Granny's visitors was Elsie Flood, a traveling lady with no real home who used to come and stay for days in Granny's small house. Elsie was unique—her coat was covered with all manner of turtle broaches, and she carried a live box turtle in her dress who she said was her friend.

I cannot remember that Granny ever asked me much of anything about myself; she did not ignore me either, she just never pried. What she had was a sparkle in her eye, lines of wisdom etched in her face, a remarkable calmness of spirit, and an unspoken faith that went to the core of her spirit and to the heart of God. It did not happen all at once—no experience of being hit over the head by the Holy Spirit—but I was powerfully struck with the conviction that whatever faith Granny had, I wanted that faith and I wanted that religion. Through Granny's hospitality evening after evening I met the living God, and the course of my life was transformed by it.

■ ■ ■

Hospitality of the highways and byways is slightly different in that it can come from perfect strangers. Alone and uncertain as to what line to take in a Kyoto subway station, where all the Japanese signs are incomprehensible, a man appears who walks me to the train I need. He waits with me until it arrives, then joins his hands as if in prayer, bows, and bids me well. Swimming in the fall along the rocky coast of the Mediterranean I glance behind me where a steamship has just passed and see a huge, ten-foot wave rapidly approaching. An old man on the shore sees the wave and feels my panic. He leaps into the water, swimming furiously toward me. He takes my hand, tells me to take a big breath, hold it, and duck. The wave rolls over us. Others follow, and as each wave arrives the man repeats the direction—breathe in, hold it, duck. Finally back in the rocky cave, he pours me a cup of steaming tea from his Thermos and laughs off his kindness. This man saved my life and I do not even know his name.

When I first arrived in Paris to live, it quickly became apparent that my high school French was not adequate for even the simplest tasks, like answering ads for an apartment, arranging to have a telephone installed, and, worst of all, answering it. I walked through my neighborhood's open-air markets with their delectable stalls of meats, fish, colorful fruit all neatly stacked, dozens of varieties of olives and cheeses from every region; I admired but did not stop. A supermarket has one distinct advantage for the foreigner—everything is set out and labeled, with prices clearly visible. After a few weeks of French lessons I took the plunge and gave myself up to the hospitality of stall keepers, who patiently listened to my atrocious accent and helped me to get exactly what I wanted. They gave me tastes of their grapes, slices of succulent melon, tangerines. "Sweet enough?" And cheeses. "Do you want this camembert for tonight or tomorrow? If you want it for tonight you'd better take the soft wheel." At the bakery it was the same and also at the butcher's and fish market: patient, helpful people going out of their way to help this inarticulate American put dinner on the table.

Told by the city that they had to cut down the diseased hedge that divided their house from the sidewalk in their St. Paul, Minnesota neighborhood, Diane and Paul decided to build a bench. "We just decided to do it. The school bus stops here at the corner of Lincoln and Dale. Mothers wait for their kids. There is a shelter for abused women down the street; this is a mixed neighborhood with lots of apartments. Sure, the kids walk on the wall and trample the flowers, but we don't care." When the Jacobsons were building the bench and the low wall behind it, one of the mothers seemed surprised and asked, "You're going to build a bench for us? Did someone die? I thought someone had to die to have a bench built!" Diane laughed and, in keeping with her role as an Old Testament scholar, wrote a poem that is printed beside the bench:

Good neighbors: Come and linger here
Let laughter fill the air!
Then Sarah laughed when she did
welcome angels unaware.

Friends who came to visit us in Paris took the wrong Metro back to their hotel by the airport. By the time they discovered their mistake, the system had closed down for the night and they were stranded until a stranger appeared and gave them a ride home. A stranger helps fix a flat tire along the interstate; another takes off her coat to cover an elderly woman who has collapsed on the busy sidewalk, just as St. Martin of Tours gave half of his cloak to the beggar at Amiens. A passerby pulls a little boy back on the sidewalk just as he is about to step out into Broadway traffic. When traveling in Kurdistan, my children were given rides by strangers and invited to meals in isolated villages. I recently flew into Cleveland and decided to take the "Rapid" into the city center, where I hoped to find a taxi. As I emerged from the train at Tower City, a fellow traveler asked me where I was going. When I told her I was headed for the Cleveland Clinic Guest House, she told me she worked there and would give me a ride. In parting she promised to take me back to Tower City and the airport when I was ready to return home. Diane was a complete stranger, but she reached out to me with a warmth and a welcome to her city and a true sense of hospitality of the highways and byways.

Accounts of help and nurture along the way are legion, among them the story of Jesus' feeding of the five thousand with five loaves and two fish. "They all ate and had enough," Luke's gospel tells us, "and the disciples took up twelve baskets of what was left over" (9:17). Perhaps the miracle lay in the fact that in the presence of Jesus, everyone dug into their packs and shared freely, captivated by divine generosity. St. Martin is said to have had a vision of Christ just at the moment he was cutting off his cloak to share with the stranger. So may we when we share hospitality of the highways and byways, seeking to serve the holy God of the universe.

▪   ▦   ▥

Another form of hospitality is so basic, so fundamental, so *usual* that it is seldom understood for what it is. This is the type of hospitality I will call the hospitality of the heart. This is a warm smile, a look of recognition, a gesture, a hug perhaps—or as one experiences so often in Japan, a look in the eye along with a slight bowing of the head with hands briefly folded in prayer, a gesture that says in effect that "I recognize and I value you as a human being, and I honor your presence right now." How often has a smile made your day? A small six-year-old reached out and gave me a big hug as I was returning to my seat in church after communion recently. This same child was part of a group of clergy families who had a small audience with Pope John Paul II. In his halting English the Pope struggled to say a few words to the church leaders, his voice heavy, almost incomprehensible and devoid of affect. Afterwards, when the children were invited to come forward for a blessing, in a flash Nicholas leapt into the Pope's lap, eliciting a wide smile as he was enveloped in John Paul's arms. It was the only time I noticed the Pope smile during the entire audience. This truly was a moment of hospitality of the heart and all of the audience was enriched by it, probably most of all, the Pope.

I might have been away for six months, but whenever I enter Herman's, Jane Bittman's diner in Colchester, Connecticut, Jane always takes a minute between working the grill and pouring coffee for her regular customers lining the counter to inquire how things are going. Or I can just drive up to the Coffee Connection at Salem Four Corners, the only four-way traffic light in my little town. The woman at the speaker phone recognizes my husband's voice and knows exactly who he is and how he likes his coffee, which she hands to him with a smile as he drives up to the window. Next door at Shows to Go, Pam and Karen always give us a big welcome, inquire after our scattered children, and know our taste in movies exactly. When Karen got married, with the reception in Pam's backyard, I felt honored to be among the small number of guests, mostly other workers at the video store. Across the street at Salem Prime Cuts, John, the owner, always manages to get me the Thanksgiving or Christmas turkey that I invariably forget to order until a few days before the festivals. These are just a few of what writer Kathleen

Norris calls in *The Cloister Walk* the eruptions of grace into our lives.

In these most basic ways we meet Jesus through the sharing of our being, through our attitudes and thoughts, through our feelings and conversations, through our bearing and behaving, through smiles and hugs and gentle bows. We meet Jesus through people whose names we will never know, and also through those with whom we work whose homes and families we will never know. The meeting may take place in an instant, in the twinkling of the eye—or over a lifetime. It can take place over the Internet: no one can calculate just how many people every day receive strength and support in coping with difficult health issues by e-mail or list servs, are given help in holding marriages together, in raising their children and, yes, in avoiding suicide. Kathleen Norris recounts her experience of visiting an ill, elderly man with a hideously bruised face who radiated such love that Norris was moved to just stand there and say to him, "It's a sweet life." Norris writes that this stranger "powerfully demonstrated to me the incarnational nature of Christian faith, how, to paraphrase Teresa of Avila, we are the only eyes, mouth, hands, feet and heart that Christ has on earth."[27]

Such are the hospitalities of the home and hearth, of the highways and byways, and of the heart by which the human community is built, nourished, and enriched. Such is the hospitality by which we live a passionate spirituality, vibrantly engaged in the heart of our everyday lives.

8

Money Talks

Given the wealth and consumerism of our culture, if we don't look at the question as to how we use our money, we have probably not explored what a right relationship with God is.

—Courtney Bourns

It was the Fourth of July and my parents had taken me to the local yacht club in the small, coastal town where I lived north of Boston. The event was the club's annual Independence Day barbecue, and after a few hours with no hamburgers or hot dogs yet in sight but plenty of beer, the normally sedate wealthy New Englanders got lively and noisy. I particularly remember the antics of Mr. Adams, I'll call him, a lean, dark-haired, and handsome man with a mischievous glint in his eye, always the life of the party. In this particular stunt, Mr. Adams leapt up on the banister of the stairs leading to the clubhouse porch and with arms outstretched and a beer can in each hand, he attempted to walk its length, balancing like a trapeze artist. His friends loved it and cheered him on. It seemed as if they could not get enough of it, and the more they yelped the more Mr. Adams danced on the rail. It all seemed strange behavior to me and I asked my mother what was going on. "Mr. Adams is drunk," was all she said. She could see that an adult so out of control was disturbing to me, so our family left the party early. As my parents bid their friends farewell, Mr. Adams was still laughing and shouting and challenging others to walk the rail.

The next morning, my mother, looking unusually serious, told me to sit down because she had something to tell me. Mr. Adams, driving home from the party, ran over a pedestrian on Lafayette Street and killed him instantly. I was young so I was not privy to the details, but the incident made me wonder. . . . Did Mr. Adams's wealthy and socially prominent family buy off the precinct captain? Did they buy the silence of the press? Did they engage the services of the best Boston lawyer money could buy? I do not know the answer to any of these questions. All I know is that a man died, that Mr. Adams did not spend even one night in jail, that the press never reported the accident, and that Mr. Adams was driving around town the next day just as if nothing had happened.

I have never been quite the same since that memorable Fourth of July, for even as a green seven-year-old, I learned in a flash just what money can buy—and that moreover, the combination of class, power, and money could be deadly. Money is so alluring that not only will nations go to war for it, but women will marry for it, and men will get away with murder because of it. Mr. Adams gave me a short course about what money will buy, and my life has been profoundly affected by it ever since.

■ ▦ ▒

Money has been a great paradox from time immemorial. Money is never neutral. It is the root of evil and it is a blessing. It enslaves and it liberates; it buys voice and it buys silence. Money is the handmaiden of power. Whoever has more can buy more, can control more. The quest for money was the driving force that sent the Spanish to steal the treasure of the Aztecs, that drove the Forty-niners to seek gold at Sutter's Creek, that sent the French, the British, the Dutch, and the Belgians to comb the mineral resources of Africa. Money and power drove Europeans to colonize the world, and even though most of the virgin land is gone and the indigenous owners have been killed or forced into submission, economic colonialism has continued to drive the wheels of power. The quest for "yellow gold" has been replaced by the rush for "black gold." Who cares what environmental damage the pursuit for oil ravages on lands and seas or how many innocent people and cultures are killed in wars for control of oil fields to power Western economies?

The quest for money knows no end. It shapes people and nations, building some up and destroying others. Money is both cosmic and personal. It seems to me that an important element of our spirituality is to look at our personal attitudes and feelings about the money we have and, just as importantly, at how our nation spends its money.

Several weeks ago I participated in a session of our local church's Bible study on the Beatitudes in Luke's gospel. Our leader gave a brief introduction and then asked the group to consider the meaning of these verses. As we began, there was a discernable hush in the room. The participants were getting stuck on the first: "How blessed are you who are poor, for yours is the kingdom of God" (Luke 6:20). Members of the group, almost all of them retired and comfortably off, some quite wealthy, sat quietly as they pondered that passage. One member asked, "Well, isn't there someplace else in the Bible where the word 'poor' is rendered as 'spiritually poor'?" The pastor acknowledged that while that was true in Matthew 5:3, tonight we were dealing with Luke's interpretation.

After a little more silence the rest of us began to speak up: "We can't really help it that we live in a rich land in a poor world." "Isn't it a matter of our *attitude* toward our wealth that's most important?" "We Americans are generous." "We can't really do anything about an unequal world economic system, can we?" A woman with a perfectly modulated, cut-glass, upper-class voice remarked, "Capitalism is just the way the world works." Another pondered, "Does this really mean that our reward is now, right here enjoying our wealth, whereas if we were poor, our reward would be in heaven?" A kind-faced woman with a wistful look admitted, "I may be well off but I don't feel happy." The pastor was still as the thoughts gathered around the table. Finally Molly remarked defensively, "I guess I live in La-la Land and I'm going to close my eyes to the rest of the world and just enjoy it!" And at that, Nancy, who had contributed little so far, came back with, "I think that poor is just what it says, *poor,* and we have to deal with it."

I can assure you that I spent the week pondering the Beatitudes and thinking about money. They led me to the story of the rich young man in Luke's gospel who asks Jesus what he needs to do to inherit eternal life (Luke 18:18–27). He tells Jesus that he has indeed kept all the commandments ever since his youth. The sorrow of this young man leaps off the Bible page, and I can feel it. I picture an earnest young person who genuinely wants to do the right thing, who wants to be in union with God. Jesus listens to him sympathetically but reminds him that there is still one more thing he must do—sell everything he has and distribute his wealth to the poor. Seeing how dejected he is, how his heart sinks, Jesus assures him that if he gives everything away in order to follow Jesus he will have riches in heaven. The rich young man goes away, disappointed, and Jesus observes to those around him, "How hard it is for the wealthy to enter the kingdom of God! It is easier for a camel to go through the eye of a needle than for someone who is rich to enter the kingdom of God" (Luke 18:24–25).

Money is such a powerful force it can change the course of human events, along with the lives of those who use it to the greater good of the community. Although I was negatively affected by money at an early age, I still admire those with wealth who use it altruistically, often at personal sacrifice. Several names come to mind. Eugene Lang, a wealthy New Yorker, decided to share his wealth with the students of the elementary school he himself had graduated from. So in 1981 he adopted a class at Public School 121 and guaranteed that each pupil would have the means to go on to some form of higher education. To help them achieve their goals he provided tutors, mentors, and all kinds of cultural enrichment. He called the project "I Have a Dream," and now, as a fruit of Lang's original investment of himself and his funds, the I Have a Dream Program has grown to include one hundred eighty projects in sixty-four cities across the United States, helping some fourteen thousand five hundred children realize their dreams for higher education.

In a similar way, Millard Fuller, who had made a fortune in business, established a housing program in 1976 which became known as Habitat for Humanity. Fuller had everything money could buy: two thousand acres of land, lakes, hundreds of head of cattle and horses, boats, an expensive home, a vacation home, and luxury cars, but his personal life was in shreds. Since he had spent all his time and energy making money at the expense of all else, virtually everything in his personal life suffered, especially his relationships with his wife and children. His wife left him and agreed to return only if he would leave the business that had made him so wealthy and start a new life. The rest is history. The Fullers drastically rescaled their lives, gave almost everything away but one car, and established Habitat for Humanity, which ultimately would provide housing for thousands of low-income people the world over.

These are but two dramatic examples of very wealthy people who have used their money to ameliorate suffering and to redress the economic imbalances in the world village. I am not talking about how they made their money—although how people make their money is just as important as how they spend it and a whole separate subject in itself. Eugene Lang and Millard Fuller are cited as striking examples of how each and every one of us can use our funds, however modest or vast they may be, to enrich the common good *and* as a means of spiritual growth. Here the widow who gives her mite is just as important in God's eyes as the person who gives millions.

■　▓　▓

Let's talk about the personal aspects of money. How do I want my money to talk? How will I use my money to build up the community, to promote justice, and to alleviate human want? Where will my money do the most good? What can I learn from the people and programs I want to support? How much money do I want to give away, and how much is enough for myself and my household to live on? In confronting these questions I take some solace in the fact that although Luke's gospel says it is hard for the wealthy to enter the kingdom of God (Luke 18:25), he does not say it is impossible.

How much money is enough? Some, like monastics and members of the Catholic Worker Movement, choose voluntary poverty and hold all their goods in common. Likewise, some indigenous cultures consider sharing to be the highest value. On Mili, a remote atoll in the Marshall Islands, for example, people live off fish from the lagoon and the fruit of their small gardens. The Marshallese who are most highly regarded members of their community are those who give the most away because the intangible value of giving comes before the value of having and keeping. In traditional Native American cultures like that of the Lakota, giving is a hallmark, and when a member of the tribe dies, all of his or her possessions are dispersed in what is known as a "give away." In these cultures having less confers a certain amount of status.

While children begin making value judgments from almost the first day of their lives, nonetheless they often possess a refreshing openness to seeing the world from a variety of perspectives. One day the father of a very wealthy family decided to take his son on a trip to the country to show him how poor people and the less fortunate live. The boy spent a couple of days and nights on the farm of a very poor family, and on his return from their trip, the father asked his son, "How was the trip?"

"It was great, Dad."

"Did you see how poor people live?"

"Yes," replied the son.

"So, tell me," asked the father, "what did you learn from the trip?"

The son replied, "I saw that we have one dog, and they have four. They also have cats that live in the barn and chickens and sheep and goats. We have a swimming pool that reaches to the middle of our yard, and they have a creek that has no end. We have imported lanterns in our yard that come on at dusk, and they have the stars to light up the night. Our patio reaches to the swimming pool, and they have the whole horizon. We have a small piece of land to live on, and they have fields beyond fields that go beyond sight. We have servants who serve us, but they serve others. We buy our food, but they grow theirs. We have walls around our property and an electronic security system to protect us, and they have friends to protect them."

The boy's father was speechless. Then his son added, "Thanks, Dad, for showing me how poor we are!"

■   ■   ■

One example of how ordinary people, following the dictates of their conscience, can work to alleviate human suffering is right under my own roof. While we were living in Europe, especially in Paris and Rome, Jeffery encountered many people who had risked their lives to flee the poverty, tyranny, war, and terror of their countries of origin to find their way to Europe. Anslem and Jude are Sri Lankans and political refugees who fled the country they love to escape the constant fear of their children stepping on land mines planted by the thousands. Now French citizens, they dearly miss their homeland and the family they left behind. Ming, a Filipina who has lived in Paris illegally for ten years, works as a maid in order to send money home to Mindanao to support her five children, as well as her brothers, sisters, and aunts. Her youngest child was only nine months old when she went to France; now he is almost ten years. The chief highlight of her month is speaking with them on the telephone, and she longs for the day when she will be a citizen and her family can be united; in the meantime, she lives every day with the fear of being picked up on the streets of Paris and sent home. Tuana, an Iraqi Kurd who runs a refugee center in Rome in the basement of the Church of St. Paul's Within the Walls, escaped by car to Iran and from there walked to Turkey with two companions, under the cover of night. Once in Turkey the friends split up, and Tuana found a place in a very crowded truck headed to Germany. He does not know where exactly he landed, nor does he know the whereabouts of his friends.

After we returned from Europe Jeffery was still haunted by the stories of Anslem and Jude, Ming and Tuana. Why should anyone be forced to leave their homes for jobs or political asylum, or out of fear they would be killed if they did not flee? He became convinced that there was a way to use his resources to address poverty, war, and injustice, but wondered, "What can one person do?" What could *he* do? Finally he picked up the phone to speak with three like-minded friends, and the result, three years later, was Episcopalians for Global Reconciliation. The four friends began by adopting for themselves the United Nations Millennium Goals (MDGs), part of the UN Millennium Declaration adopted by the leaders of 189 nations at the Millennium Summit held in New York City in September 2000. The eight goals include the eradication of extreme hunger and poverty; the achievement of universal primary education; the promotion of gender equality; the reduction of childhood mortality; improving women's health; combating HIV/AIDS, malaria, and other diseases; ensuring environmental sustainability; and the development of a global partnership for development. The figure set by the world leaders to realize these goals was 0.7 percent of each nation's gross national product.

For these four people, all of them busy and none of them wealthy, trying to find a way to begin to implement the goals was a tall order. Their first action was to pledge a percentage of each of their incomes to overseas programs and projects. The second was to involve the church through the creation of Episcopalians for Global Reconciliation (EGR). Now as the group approaches its third birthday, they have a lot to show for their work: The General Convention of the Episcopal Church has adopted the Millennium Development goals and 0.7 percent giving; almost half of the church's dioceses have also done so in some form. There have been large gatherings around the country, and the consciousness of thousands has been aroused. EGR's Steering Committee believes that thousands of dollars have been donated to all kinds of programs and projects in the poorest parts of the world.[28]

How have others responded to the question Jeffery asked himself, "What can one person do?" What have they done to make a difference, and how do they feel about it? Recently I interviewed Lallie Lloyd, who grew up in a comfortable family that supported the arts, cultural institutions, and hospitals through regular giving and through participation on their boards. As a child she did not think of herself as wealthy, and it was not until the 1960s on visits to her grandmother's large house in suburban Philadelphia that she became aware of the racial and economic tensions building just a few miles away in the ghettos of the inner city. Neither her grandmother nor her parents talked much about it, but Lallie looked at television, read the daily paper, and knew that something was drastically wrong: "I was about twelve at the time, and I remember thinking that we had more than we needed. We just didn't need all of this." It was a revelatory moment, and she began to educate herself about issues of justice and poverty. She still respects the ideals of simple charity that her parents set for their children, but came to see things differently. Generous as their giving was, most of it perpetuated the status quo, while she herself was passionate about "transformative justice." She was motivated partly by guilt, but far stronger was "an overwhelming sense of being blessed to have what I have. This abundance was given to me by God not for my own use, but to share with others." Later she began to work on urban public school reform after she and her husband became resident directors of a program that brought seven urban African American teenaged girls to Guilford, Connecticut to attend the local high school, thus doubling its minority population. They became a family for a year, sharing their lives together, household chores, meals, holidays, leisure, weekends, evenings of conversation. It was an education for the girls, but even more so for Lallie. Through these teenagers she was introduced to a world very different from her own, and began to question why it was that they had to leave their inner-city communities in order to get a good high school education.

Lallie says that her giving grows in proportion to her faith: "When I have the money to give away, I look at what needs help *right now*. I try to make a meaningful connection between my faith, my life of abundance, and my giving." The habit of tithing, giving away ten percent of her income, "has increased my sense of gratitude for what I have, and it becomes a spiritual challenge to grow into more generosity." She feels that the spiritual impact of the tithe is to increase our sense of gratitude, which may be one of the reasons our Jewish and Christian forebears regarded it as essential. Her expenditures are intentional and, at their best, transformative—they transform her faith as well as the programs, causes, and projects she adopts. In summary, she says, "I don't feel that much of what I am came from me. I was incredibly lucky to be born into the family I was. I can see the hand of God in everything, and that is a humbling and wonderful insight."

By profession, Judith Lockhart-Radtke is both a social worker and a midwife who has also studied nursing. Her initial desire was to help women both at home and in developing nations. Through Oxfam America and Grassroots International she visited women in their communities, grassroots clinics, and cottage industries on five continents, and everywhere she went she was impressed by the many instances of women helping women. In Vietnam, for instance, she met with a group of women who wanted to start a poultry and pig project, and each received twenty dollars from an aid organization. Judith was moved to see that, from the start, the women made the decision to put aside one dollar each to help when someone might need it, especially to restock if their chickens became sick and died. If these women who had so little were so eager to be generous, Judith felt that this was a message to her.

At the age of sixty, she traveled through the mountains of the Oaxaca region of Mexico, its second poorest state, where twelve indigenous groups live in lovely and sometimes remote villages. Traveling through the region on horseback, she soon saw that health care was desperately needed, particularly a birthing center, as well as a way for the women to support themselves financially. To meet both needs, Judith joined with a Swiss midwife who lives in Oaxaca, Pia Scognamiglia, to establish the Circle of Women. Pia began the birthing center, and Judith developed a weaving project with women in three communities. There are now forty-six of them, and they make beautiful shawls, pillowcases, and table designs of wool and cotton that are sold through an American distributor and over the Internet.

As the women have begun to make money, they are experiencing a new self-confidence and a continuing desire to help themselves. Only six of the weavers know how to read, and now the Circle of Women is exploring various literacy programs. Judith visits Oaxaca about four times a year, sometimes staying as long as four to six weeks. She readily admits that it has been a struggle at times, but starting the Circle of Women from the beginning has been the opportunity of a lifetime. First she was motivated by the need to take action; later she saw the spiritual dimension of it. It all began with her belief that women can learn to take leadership and realize the possibilities of their lives. "It started with my belief in women. Only later, as I reflected, did I realize that this has something to do with what it means to be a Christian. As I've read

Archbishop Desmond Tutu and Mother Teresa everything has come together—working alongside women, action, and the evolution of my faith."

■   ■   ■

And what about the rest of us, who are swamped by the all-pervasive consumer culture bombarding us with messages about what we need to have and to buy in order to be happy? When so much new home construction is devoted to building oversized houses with three- and four-car garages, it is a challenge to remain satisfied with an ordinary house. When my six-year-old grandson was riding with me around the small rural town where we live, he noticed several trailer houses and very modest one- or two-bedroom dwellings, and asked, "How can people live in these tiny homes?" At such a young age he has already internalized the message that bigger is better, that more is necessary. He goes to school with children who know that if they want something—whatever it may be—their parents will buy it. While his parents try to counter this ethos, by doing so they are profoundly at odds with the surrounding culture where every billboard, television commercial, magazine, and junk mailing entices us to buy.

How much do we need? Gregory F. Augustine Pierce, in his book *Spirituality@Work,* suggests:

> One simple discipline is to admit that we already have enough. . . . This discipline would simply be a matter of reminding ourselves regularly that we have been blessed with whatever material possessions we have, that there are lots of people who are less fortunate than we are, and that for the most part we are making ends meet. This may take the form of a simple daily prayer, or a plaque or saying at our workplace that reminds us that we have enough."[29]

But he also concedes that merely being satisfied with what we already have is not sufficient; we also have to confront our *desire* to have more things and more money. We have to "decide what is enough and then stick to it in order to save our very souls."

This is far from easy. Right now I am looking out my back door at the place where I would really like to have a deck. It is close to the kitchen, and I can foresee easy, lazy summer meals under the trees. We do not need the deck—we have other places to sit outside—but I have been thinking about it for years. Every time I get ready to call the carpenter, however, I hold back. I cannot feel good about spending $5,000 on something we do not really need. I know I would feel even better if I would just make a decision to forget the deck and send the money to support Habitat for Humanity in Guatemala or Judith's weavers in Mexico. I am also a little angry with myself for getting stuck on something so frivolous when I know that such a question is pure luxury in a world of want. While we try to be responsible with our funds and carefully think through what we want to give away and to whom, we probably do not give away nearly enough and we have certain blind spots. And, to be honest, we tend to console ourselves with what we *do* give away and ignore some of the nagging issues. Like the deck.

Nonetheless, I know that if I am going to maintain a vibrant faith, hard questions about money have to be asked and answered. If you are like me, perhaps you will join me in asking a few hard questions such as these:

■   How much money is enough? How much do I really need to keep for myself and my family?

■   What addictions does my money feed, such as spending, shopping, the appearance of success, luxury, power, control?

■   Where does my money come from? Do I benefit from systems that oppress others? What kinds of seeds are my investments growing in the world?

▪ How does my faith direct the use of my money?
What people, causes, movements, programs, political
candidates would I like my money to support?

▪ What messages do I want to give to my children and
grandchildren about my use of money?

▪ Do our children really need the money we want to
give them? Are there others who need it more?

▪ How can we open up a conversation about money
with members of our families, our communities, and our
churches?

▪ How much is left over after we have done our giving? How can we live on less and give more and still live
in this culture?

We cannot brush off these questions. If we have been educated beyond high school, if we have jobs, insurance, and
retirement packages, if we own our own home or can comfortably afford a rental, we are wealthy. Most of you are probably not millionaires but are more like me, worrying about
whether or not to build the deck in the back of the house.
Wherever we are on the continuum between "getting by" and
wealthy, the answers we give to questions of wealth and the
actions that flow from them might just, as Pierce suggests, save
our very souls.

▪   ▪   ▪

Daring to find a right relationship with our money *and* a right
relationship with God, daring to take the plunge, will be
nothing other than liberating. Once the hurdles of thinking
about the just use of money are overcome, and you begin to
align your use of money with your most deeply held values,
you may be transformed—eager to help others come to terms
with their money and make their money talk for them. Joan
Martin, a very wealthy woman, is one of those who has
become converted to making her money talk. Facing the
issues of her vast wealth and directing some of it to causes
close to her heart, such as a hospital for homeless men in

Washington and programs to aid the poorest of the poor in Haiti, has transformed her life:

> I feel as though God taps me on the shoulder, then I just know. And I am not doing it impulsively. I am doing it out of a deep knowing that this is what I am supposed to do. I never know when these moments are going to come up or how they're going to come or in what form. But they give me great joy.

Learning to face the meaning of money in her life has taken Joan Martin a long time, for her wealth had isolated her from others and there was a long dry period in her life when she could not find herself. Now she says:

> Some of my moneyed friends wonder why I'm so happy. I have learned that it isn't enough just to write a check. You have to have the courage and the discipline to become involved. I have been asked the question, "How much is enough?" I don't know the answer to that yet. But when it comes to struggles with money and places with untold opportunities to make a difference, I somehow keep coming back for more. Is this perhaps freedom?[30]

Money talks, but what does it say? The well-being of the world and our own passionate engagement with life prompts us to look money squarely in the eye and decide how we are going to make it talk for us.

9

Rushing for Justice

I have learned that it is not enough to espouse a position or point of view merely verbally (even though it may, in fact, be a good one) and expect it to be listened to and accepted at face value. For it to be credible and influential, the point of view must be personally embodied, given practical, lifestyle support. It is the day-to-day living out of our beliefs which carry weight and have moral authority.

—Richard Steele, South African conscientious objector

Right now I am taking a moment to look at what I am wearing, from the bottom up. On my feet are sandals that were designed and assembled in Germany, their soles a combination of rubber from an African rubber plantation and leather from Argentina. The steel buckles were made from iron and carbon, mined from somewhere under the earth. My jeans were made in the USA in a unionized garment factory. The cotton T-shirt I am wearing is so old I cannot read the label—I hope it was not made in a Chinese sweatshop where garment workers are paid two cents for each shirt assembled, but the odds are that's exactly where it came from. My lambswool sweater was made in Scotland from the wool of sheep grazing on the moors and bought secondhand in an OXFAM charity store. The origin of the jeans and the sweater are straightforward and I can feel all right about wearing them, but I wonder about the buckles on the sandals, the rubber on the soles, and the T-shirt. These garments are the products of the labor of others, some of it just and some unjust. Human beings have been a part of every stage of everything I am wearing, from its raw source in nature to the salespeople who sold them to me. So even before I leave my home in the morning, there are ample reasons to give thanks for the lives of others by whose labors I am clothed.

Or let's get even more basic: we are all here because someone gave us the gift of life and cared for and nurtured us. As human beings we are born into community, and we live our lives by the grace and mercy of others. Our sense of the other is as basic as the day we were born and as cosmic as the soles of my shoes taken from an African rubber tree. A spirituality of everyday life in today's world is first of all marked by a sense of indebtedness and thanksgiving for everything tangible and intangible that we have been given by others. It is nurtured among those closest to us, in our families and households and through participation in our communities, in the affairs of our nation and our world and especially in giving ourselves to serving the poor.

▪   ▪   ▪

To the question "What does God require?" the Old Testament prophet Micah answers that it is first of all to do justice. Doing justice takes many forms; it extends from where we buy our clothes and the food we put on our dining table to our participation in politics and the public life of our communities. People work for justice through the system of elected office and through participation in community affairs; they do so individually as well, by taking a stand in their places of employment and in the street holding up a protest banner. Both individual and corporate efforts for justice are essential in building up the common good.

I realize it is not fashionable now to suggest that people of faith are called to work through the political process. Politics has become a dirty word, and many politicians have shame-lessly used religion as a tool to further the narrow, selfish aims of a small but influential class of people working for their own personal gain. But that is a corruption of politics. It is still through politics—however tarnished—that we guard God's world and God's creatures everywhere, and it is through pol-itics that we care for the common good. Furthermore, a vibrant faith calls for our passionate engagement in the affairs of this world; it means turning outward to all the pain, the complexity, the injustice, the suffering we see around us and on the nightly news and taking our part in doing something about it. What we do *does* matter. What I have bought and am wearing today, or have decided against buying or wearing, matters. Even an action as small as casting a vote can make a difference: in my small town of thirty-eight hundred people, candidates and referenda frequently win and lose by just one or two votes.

I know a lot of politicians. Because of their work, libraries are built, children are educated, the poor find affordable hous-ing, forests are protected, communities, states, and nations are run in an orderly fashion. Politicians work hard, often to the detriment of their personal and family lives. They do not have a lot of evenings and weekends free, and their work is often thankless. I decided to use just one of them as an illustration of what the political life is like, how it is formed and how it expresses itself in legislation that makes a difference to peo-ple's lives. I wanted to talk to a working politician, grounded in the local district but with eyes open to the nation and the world, a person of lively faith whose actions are guided by belief. So I decided to spend a few hours talking to Massachusetts State Representative Byron Rushing in his office at the State House in hopes that he would tell me something about faith and commitment in the political sphere.

When I arrived at Byron's office and his secretary called him off the floor of the House, it was as if a whirlwind had entered the room. He told me he didn't have time for lunch, and he hoped that I wouldn't mind if the public address system from the floor of the chamber was turned on because he would have to listen and be ready to go out and vote. After he sat down—a vigorous, energetic, and passionate man with a quick intellect and a wide smile—he talked nonstop for two hours, except for the two times he left to vote. When he returned each time he continued exactly where he had left off

"Today," he told me, "we are debating a constitutional amendment in order to make health care a right and not a privilege. It almost certainly would be voted on affirmatively, so a tactic by those opposed will be to try to stop it coming up to a vote in the first place. There are other amendments I plan to vote against. It may seem strange that I have to work on the wording of an amendment that I'm going to vote against, but if you are not going to win, you want to influence how you lose.

"Civil rights and human rights are my priorities. I always push the envelope on how the state understands civil rights and legislates protection for human beings. Once you start doing things people learn your priorities and they start coming to you about civil and human rights. So it's not just what I'm thinking about, it's what people bring to me. People who are interested in human rights in other countries come to me, such as the students who were running a campaign against Pepsi-Cola in Burma. They came because of my work in the antiapartheid movement and divestment in South Africa, beginning in the 1970s. In the 1970s anti-apartheid groups were getting behind the Sullivan Principles describing how business was to be conducted in South Africa, but many, including me, didn't think we were putting enough pressure on South Africa or the U. S. government. In order to break the apartheid system we had to damage the South African economy and get major companies to leave South Africa. So this began the divestment movement, and churches, universities, and the public all got behind it. But a large untouched area was state pension funds. Since the state of Massachusetts is a consumer, we should be able to use our funds to make a statement. If state pension plans invested in companies doing business in South Africa could divest, this would create a large hole in the South African economy. Both Connecticut and Massachusetts' legislatures voted to divest funds, and this was the first time state pension funds were used politically. We had $30 billion in pension funds for state workers, so this divestment action made quite an impression in South Africa and took a decisive role in bringing the government down."

Byron says he cannot state the time or the day when he first became passionate about social justice, but it happened very close to home. Like Phillips Brooks, the great Broad Church preacher and espouser of social causes who became passionate because of the influence of an aunt in Teaneck, New Jersey, Rushing acquired his passion for justice from his mother, whom he called "quietly progressive." Raised by his mother in the Episcopal Church, they attended an integrated church in Syracuse. Rushing also learned progressive ideas at a summer camp in the Adirondacks for Universalists, Unitarians, and members of Ethical Culture. "Diversity and free thinking were important to them, and so they recruited Asians and blacks, like me! I went to the camp every summer from the eighth through the eleventh grades, and I was greatly influenced by their intellectual criticism of Christianity. This was okay with my mother. My mother was a solid Episcopalian, but her position was that I could believe anything, just so long as I went to church. If I didn't want to receive communion, it was okay with her. If I had some doubts about the creed, it didn't worry her. But I had to go to church! In retrospect I think I would have been helped if my priest could have admitted, 'Hey, I have my doubts too.' But, you know, this is something the clergy don't really do."

He went to Harvard during the civil rights years. At the end of his junior year he had planned to go south to work for the movement, but when a new chapter of the Congress for Racial Equality (CORE) was established in Syracuse he decided to stay home and volunteered. "In Syracuse I could be an inside agitator, and I felt this would be more useful than being an outside agitator, as I would have been in the South. This was 1963, the summer of the March on Washington and Martin Luther King's 'I Have a Dream' speech. Actually I thought the planners of the march were a little too conservative, and I thought it would be a better idea for us to close down the urban renewal in the city of Syracuse for the day. So I got them to stop tearing down the building they were working on. There was a little violence, but it was necessary to let people know that you can't eliminate discrimination by just clearing slums. The roots of discrimination are deeper than that. By this time I was fully living the concept of community organization. The idea here was that if you're going to deal with discrimination, you have to deal with systemic causes rather than individual cases of discrimination, so we had to work for political control over where black people lived and where they had their communities. One time, for instance, there was a Syracuse city bus company that wanted to set up its headquarters in the black community, in a residential area right in front of a public housing building, which was dangerous for the children—to say nothing of the unhealthy fumes from the buses."

Rushing is also a pacifist. Prior to the Vietnam War he had registered as a conscientious objector, and worked two years as an orderly at Rochester General Hospital. When he arrived back in Boston, voter registration campaigns were in progress and people from the black community were angry about the war, but they and their churches seemed powerless. "As intellectuals, we leaders tried to look at the issues historically. We looked at black writers and philosophers who advocated for autonomy, more participation, on the part of the people. I tried to figure out why black people had been so powerful in some places and also why they had become so powerless. In Boston, with my interest in the history of black movements, I read and read about the history of our people. Black people have a long history in Boston; they lived on Beacon Hill, now one of the most elite areas of the city. The first black regiment to fight in the Civil War—the Fifty-fourth—were Boston men, now memorialized in a monument across the street from the State House."

After ten years he was ready for a move and had a growing conviction that he needed to be more directly a part of the political process. In 1982 Mel King decided to run for mayor of Boston, creating a vacancy in the 9th Suffolk District; Rushing ran and won, and has been the district's representative ever since. He represents forty-five thousand people in a district that includes the South Side of Boston, Fenway, Lower Roxbury, and the Western Campus of the Massachusetts Institute of Technology. His district is sixty percent white and forty percent non-white, with African Americans, Hispanics, and a growing Asian population. It includes a large gay population, a smaller lesbian population, and the first gentrified neighborhood in the city, the South End.

"I tell my constituents that I can do anything they want that's right—just so long as I can get eighty others to agree! My major criteria for staying in the job are that I have to enjoy it and that I do things that are necessary. The content of the job is incredibly varied. It's the intellectual challenge that keeps the job fresh. This freshness comes both from the job and the people I represent. What I have learned is that you have to listen, really listen, to the people in the community in order to hear what the important issues are for them. Democracy is a relatively new idea, and for many people in this country it is an experiment. One of the most exciting things about politics is making democracy work here in the USA and around the world. For me this means trying to develop systems where every individual is empowered and whose identity is centered on being a human being first. Everything else is secondary. Every day I try to figure out how my work is focused on Jesus Christ—to understand human beings as human beings is a religious concept."

Byron Rushing is a good example of a man passionately engaged in making the world more just in his own corner of it—the 9th District of Boston—while using his influence to bring about justice far beyond, such as in South Africa and

Burma. His life story is an account of passionate engagement in the heart of the world, rushing for justice in all its forms. He has worked through government channels to sow justice and build up the common good; he has also worked outside the system, as many of us have done on occasion.

We may try to emulate a figure like Rushing and decide for a life in politics, or we may decide to try another way of being passionately involved in the world—simply by taking a stand for what we believe is right and just. We can offer our small acts of witness, insignificant in themselves, for the sake of the greater good.

■   ■   ■

Last year my local newspaper hyped the news of the upcoming "christening" of the Navy's newest, most high-tech nuclear submarine, the *Jimmy Carter,* by his wife, the former First Lady. It held a particular poignancy for me because I know some of the men and women who have built this submarine. They are neighbors of mine whose acquaintance I value; they live on my street and they serve on some of the same town committees I do. Usually I try to ignore this part of their lives. I try not to talk about it with them because I know it is their livelihood in an economy where there are not a lot of alternatives. I enjoy the harmony I share with my neighbors and I do not want to disturb it. But as I thought about the $4.4 billion price tag for this death-dealing marvel, named for Jimmy Carter, my anger reached the boiling point. How could this Nobel Peace Prize winner and former president of the United States, whose life I have admired for so long, lend his name to a submarine whose payload could annihilate thousands of people at the toss of a switch? I was angry, disheartened, and sad.

The morning of the christening arrived, the eve of the sixtieth anniversary of D-Day. My husband, planning a quiet Saturday, must have thought he was in the company of a woman possessed as I turned the basement upside down in search of posterboard and Magic Markers. As I designed my sign, "Sinful Waste in a Starving World," I calmed down a little. There were still two hours to go before the event, but with all the media attention given to the event I gave myself plenty of time to make the twenty-minute ride from my home to the shipyard in Groton and avoid the scramble for parking spaces.

I used to be a regular on the protest line whenever a new nuclear submarine was launched, but I had been away for most of the past decade and my sense of direction was hazy. Missing the turn to the fort where the peace people always gather, before I knew it I found myself in the main Electric Boat parking lot, right behind the shipyard. Many of the well-dressed guests were friends and greeted each other; there was a lightness and a sense of festivity in the air. We all walked to the entrance gate of the yard and as they went in, I stepped aside and unrolled my sign.

Immediately forty police officers converged on me, their two-way radios chattering. One of the state troopers told me where I should stand while another dozen erected police barriers around me and blocked the shipyard side of the street. And there I stood, all by myself for forty-five minutes, holding up my sign. A few children came up close to read the message, and some of them smiled and waved as their parents tugged them away. A dozen or so adults sneered at me and uttered unrepeatable comments; most of them just looked in the other direction. Rescue finally came as the line of peace people walked down the hill from the fort, many friends whom I had not seen for such a long time and who provided some company (aside from the police) on my side of the barrier.

But while I was still standing alone, I wondered, Am I just a fool standing here with a homemade sign? Is this an appropriate activity for a respectable grandmother? There is only one of me—I am outnumbered a thousand to one. Can this small protest of mine possibly do any good? Why can't I just "lighten up" and go along with the crowd? It would feel so much better. Realistically, I could acknowledge that this was, after all, just a minor action on my part. It cost me nothing except a little embarrassment and the surprise my neighbors would feel when they saw me in the Sunday paper, staring out at them from behind police barriers as they sipped their breakfast coffee.

It was just a very small protest on my part, but it was a stand against warfare and waste I felt my faith was calling me to make. In the forty-five minutes I stood alone, I got a brief taste of the way people are treated who regularly—in season and out—take a position for peace or who take a stand against the drift of the prevailing culture. My friend Cal Robertson, for example, is a Vietnam veteran who has spent the last twenty years holding up his peace signs every day in front of Electric Boat and the Submarine Base—"Non-Violence or Non-Existence" and "Remember the Children." He has been spat upon, cursed, humiliated, and last year he was run over by a truck. But he has never returned anger for anger, and there are many people, whether they agree with him or not, who are touched by his loving way of witnessing for peace. When Cal was in the hospital following his accident, members of his church volunteered to hold up his signs until he could return. Certainly many famous people have dared to take a stand— Gandhi, King, Dorothy Day—but there are thousands more whose names are known only to God.

■　　■　　■

Many searches for a living God come up empty. People seek and seek, but they do not find. They wonder why they have difficulty feeling the joy of faith, the presence of God in their lives, the certainty of believing. They take to the desert and the open road; they withdraw into retreats; they seek answers through spiritual direction from mystics, monastics, and gurus. A spiritual guide can be immensely useful but only if he or she leads the searcher to some form of service in God's world, especially for the most vulnerable. A lively spiritual quest cannot take place in a vacuum. Acts of prayer and meditation are only efficacious if the search for faith leads to the streets of life—loving the weak and those who exist on the margins, helping the poor, and taking stands for justice. For Christians, the model of faith and service is Christ. To learn the riches of God, look to the kinds of people in our day who are most like those who claimed Jesus' special attention in his. Look at the people with whom he surrounded himself, the ones he served, healed, affirmed, defended, and loved. For Christians, faithfulness in our day compels us take to our hearts the same kind of company Jesus kept. Jesus is best met in those to whom he gave special attention, people on the edges—the poor, the stranger, the immigrant, the captive, the brokenhearted, the lonely, those oppressed by prejudice and injustice, those shut out from prosperity. The poor are those who labor under a great weight, crushed, excluded, judged, and humiliated. The poor are like Jesus, who had nothing material save the clothes on his back, and ultimately even those would be snatched from him. He had no home. He was often misunderstood, even by those closest to him. He was adored by his friends but despised by the civil and religious authorities of his day. He was a person stripped of everything, even his physical existence, and like the poor, subjected to the evil of others.

Often we shrink from the poor. We turn away and try to ignore the eyes of the panhandler at Grand Central Station and the gypsy mother with her baby waving a paper coffee cup in our face out on the street. They make us feel uneasy—through their poverty we ourselves and our ways of life are called into question and judged. Without intending to, the poor hold up a mirror to us and our society. They remind us that but for the grace of God and the cushion of a regular paycheck, we too could be living on the streets. The poor remind us of our failure to care for our neighbors, along with the failure of the systems we have designed to help them.

A spirituality consistent with the values of the commonwealth of God will include works of love and nurture by which we seek to ameliorate the suffering of our neighbors.

Such outreach may take many forms, depending upon one's distinct callings, talents, and interests. It may mean volunteering in a homeless shelter or serving at the food panty, offering *pro bono* legal assistance, being a Big Brother or Big Sister to a city child who lives in the projects, or tutoring children in an afterschool program. It may include taking a stand for justice or participating in politics and public life, seeking to address the systemic causes of poverty and injustice, building houses for the poor and working to build up the common good. Everyone who searches for a vibrant faith, who thirsts for passionate engagement in God's world, will determine for themselves what actions they feel compelled to take. This may not be easy, but if we allow our hearts and minds to be open to the promptings of the spirit, it will lead us in paths of justice, love, and truth.

10

Friendship

Friend sits by friend....
They read the mysteries off each other's foreheads.

—Rumi, "A Mouse and a Frog"

Here in front of me I have two pictures of friendship, one taken in 1984 and the other in 2004. The 1984 photograph shows a dozen high school seniors and June graduates leaning against or standing on top of John Nutcher's large 1966 Pontiac *Catalina,* nicknamed "The White Horse." The photo was taken at Town House Road, the housing development in Hamden, Connecticut, a New Haven suburb, where five of the boys lived and behind which they had built a cabin and an immense skateboard half-pipe in an abandoned market garden. It is a happy picture of a band of brothers who had been friends since the seventh grade when they were all neighbors and attending the same junior high school. John Hearne is wearing the East Coast Locals T-shirt, the skateboard club the boys started and, included in the picture, are several skateboards. A few of the boys had known each other since first and second grade. This is a picture of laughing, lighthearted teenagers who look as if they didn't have a care in the world. But there is a certain poignancy there, too, because it was the day before John Hearne left home for the Navy and the last day for a long time that the group would be together again.

These "dogs," as they call themselves, were truly a band of brothers, best friends to each other through most of their formative years, together every day and all weekend long. They made their money delivering the morning newspapers in the nearby apartment buildings and at the range of fast-food restaurants along Dixwell Avenue. They were employed at the Laurel View Country Club, a municipal golf club where they worked the grill and carried golf bags. Jim got them jobs at Danny's Italian Restaurant. They did landscaping and painted houses with College Pro. They went to all the rock concerts on the New Haven green in the summer and went swimming every day and after hours in the Town House Road pool. Hank Lyon, the oldest of four boys in his family, was a Hamden policeman's son and while the boys never got into any real trouble, they always thought that if they did, Hank Senior could help them out. Their dialogue was a constant babble of jokes, accounts of shenanigans long remembered and rehashed.

None of these sixteen- and seventeen-year-olds took life too seriously, but they were with each other in times of trouble, and when John Hearne's father died suddenly, they were there to help him get through his grief. Within two months of this 1984 picture being taken, the brothers would all go their separate ways. Some would return for their last year of high school. John would join the Navy, Tim the Merchant Marine Academy, and the others would go off to various colleges and universities. John Nutcher (nicknamed "Devo" after a new wave band popular in the early 1980s) would drive off in his White Horse by himself to join a touring rock band.

Throughout their college years, the band of brothers remained close. They made an annual camping trip to Vermont, sometimes bringing their girlfriends, sometimes just by themselves. The ranger at Moosalamoo State Park made sure he placed the noisy crew far away from any other campers. They were waiters. They worked on building sites and framed houses. Chris and Pat started their own house painting company they called Fagan's Boys. About half of them worked for Joe's Landscaping where, if the work was light, Joe would take them off sailing for an afternoon. At the end of one summer he sold his boat to John Marone and Jimmy Sette. These novice sailors, after a few sailing lessons from Joe, took the boat on a cruise to Florida. Along the way they experienced storms, foul weather, and foul tempers, and by the time they reached Miami they were not speaking to each other. They sold the boat and flew home and soon patched up their friendship. Chris and John went to Europe on student rail passes, where they hiked in the Dachstein Alps of Austria and slept in shepherds' cabins high in the mountains. They visited Amsterdam and camped out in the caves on the southern coast of Crete. The tales of these trips—embellished over time—have been added to their treasury of youthful adventures.

Twenty years later, half of the original band of brothers are in the 2004 picture taken in Malibu at John Nutcher's wedding. Some of them look a little heavier, some have lost their floppy heads of hair; still, they all look fresh and vibrant. What has happened to them in the intervening twenty years? All of them have been in and out of relationships; some have gotten married and stayed married; some have married and divorced; others have never married but lived with various partners. At ages thirty-seven and thirty-eight they are well established in their careers. After his discharge from the Navy, John Hearne moved to Sacramento, began a family, and is now the sales manager of a large trucking company. Pat, a carpenter, worked in antique building restoration and is now a New York architect. John, the groom, who once played in a rock band, is now a labels manager in the music industry in Los Angeles. Mike is a senior business systems analyst in a software company in Massachusetts, a suburban dad, and a rabid Red Sox fan. Chris has been living in Kyoto, Japan, for the last dozen years, where he is a writer for Lonely Planet travel guides and travels to some of the remotest places in the world. The most entrepreneurial of the band is Jim, still the fast-talking Italian American, full of laughter, still not taking himself too seriously. Jim got into the real estate business when a lot of money could be made buying and selling condominiums. He has enough money to live anywhere in the world, but he remains the happiest in the New Haven area, surrounded by his family and close friends.

And what of the others who did not make it into the 2004 picture? Russell was lean, fast-thinking and fast-talking, a little mischievous, and a great raconteur with an irreverent, quick wit. He could have been a stand-up comic but actually became an assistant principal in a high school in North Haven, Connecticut. Perry, Russ's University of Connecticut room-mate, is now an assistant attorney general of the State of Connecticut. They are the only members of the group to have married and stayed married to their high school sweethearts. John, who was a Vassar student with Chris, is now an Otis Elevator technician living in Branford, around the corner from Jim. Andy, who studied forestry and environmental science at the University of Maine, is now a forest ranger in Virginia. Hank, the policeman's son, is now a hair dresser in Venice Beach, California. Only Alex and Tim have disappeared, and none of them seems to know where they have gone.

The glue that holds these friends together is their shared memory of good and bad times in one small neighborhood in Hamden, Connecticut. By now wives, partners, and chil-dren have all been incorporated into the group. Their lives have taken them in different directions: they do not share the same political views, they have different living situations, jobs, and professions, but they remain loyal, devoted to each other. Pat says that although he has made other friends, the bonds have not endured, while "this group is transparent and they've been very reliable, very consistent. A great deal of positive inertia was put into motion during those years in Hamden. Many of us have inspired and encouraged each other along the way, and I think we're still riding that wave."

John Hearne thinks the enduring friendship has to do with a shared memory "of all the things we did wrong and right, lending each other money when it was necessary, and a shared thirst for knowledge." He very much misses the intelligent, engaging conversations the group used to have when they were growing up together as hometown friends, acknowledging, "We've got some differing political views, but the same value systems."

"It's hard to believe we've remained close friends for over twenty years," John Nutcher marvels. "It amazes me how different we all are, yet we get along so well. We drift away and come back together, and no matter how much time goes by we are always there for each other. Sitting around telling and listening to stories for hours never gets old—even though they're the same old story half the time. The memories are priceless, and the dedication we have to each other is lifelong. The bottom line is we have fun together, we make each other laugh, we follow our own rules, and we never seem to be any older when we are together. Other than that, nothing else really matters."

■   ▓   ▓

Friendship is like hospitality in that it involves the sharing of oneself and receiving from another, but whereas hospitality may lead to friendship, it is different. Hospitality often involves the stranger, the alien, the refugee. There may be a certain risk in offering and receiving hospitality. In friendship, risk is replaced by security, an alien status is replaced by a closeness, a sense of insecurity is replaced by a feeling of belonging; the unknown quality of hospitality becomes a sense of knowing in friendship. We can ask something of friends, and they of us. We can depend upon them. Our friends love us, they support us, they correct us, they help us make choices. They come to our aid when we are down or in trouble. They listen to us with compassion. If they judge us they do so gently. Friends seek our good. They hold out a hand to us. We can call on a friend in the depth of the night. We can visit when we feel like it. With friends we drop pretense. We do not need to impress our friends. They require no front or special persona. Friends offer companionship. They are fellow travelers. Friends share joys and pleasures. With friends we dream and plan and wish and hope. We laugh a lot; sometimes we cry. When a change occurs in our life, we want to share the news immediately with our friends: I'm having a baby. I had a miscarriage. It's twins. We're splitting up. We're getting divorced. I've got a promotion. I'm changing jobs. I'm running in the New York Marathon. I won. I got elected. I got accepted to law school. We're buying a house. We're moving. My beloved had a heart attack. He died. I'm jumping on a plane. I'm coming. I'll be with you.

Last week we heard that our friend Mary was in hospice and not likely to live much longer. We have known Mary and her husband Bob ever since our early days as a family living at Union Theological Seminary; Bob was the dean of the School of Sacred Music and Mary, also a musician, was in many ways the mother of the community. She greeted all the new faculty members and their families and had a sense of knowing just what they needed. I was a green New Yorker, tired all the time with taking care of three energetic children aged four and under, and Mary often came to my aid with luscious casseroles and batches of warm, homebaked chocolate chip cookies. Eventually we all moved together to the Yale Institute for Sacred Music—a move that changed and shaped all our lives as the friendship endured. Now at age eighty-eight Mary does not have much time left.

I was apprehensive about visiting her in a hospice, a place where everyone is dying. Perhaps I was afraid it would force me to confront my own mortality a little more directly than I wanted. Perhaps I was feeling sad about losing a friend to whom we owe so much, or guilty about having lost touch over the years. I last saw Mary healthy and robust; how would I cope with seeing her on the brink of death? Would I be able to force myself through the hospice door, or would I cop out and wait in the car while my husband made the visit? My tangled thoughts pulled me in both directions as I hesitated and paced the parking lot. Should I go in? Can I do it?

I took a deep breath and went in. Mary and I had a long
and energetic conversation, filled with laughter, recalling high
points in our lives together—it was a way of thanking her for
everything she has meant to me in my life. She reminded me
of the time I took it upon myself to teach her how to make
tea "in the English way" and how chagrined she felt—everything that came out of her kitchen was supposed to be perfect! In those days wives (they were all wives then!) of
established faculty members had the power to make their
younger counterparts realize their insignificance, and we
recalled the night when we were harangued by one humor-
less crone who admonished us to use butter when making our
cakes for our meetings, never margarine. It was a silly, easy
conversation, and it was almost inconceivable to me that
Mary was so close to death. Part of me could not believe such
easy conversation would not go on forever; another part fully
understood this to be the final parting. I consciously tried to
fix Mary's image in my mind so I would remember her warm
smile forever.

■   ■   ■

What is the role of friendship in our lives, and how do friends
contribute to a rich spirituality of the everyday? How do we
seek and serve God in our friendships? Some friendships
build slowly over time; others take place in an instant. But
whether friendship has evolved quickly or slowly, if it is going
to continue, a spark—an energy—has to be struck between
both partners. A test of whether the friendship is authentic is
how quickly friends get on each other's "wave length" when
they have been apart for a while.

People change. Life is not static. Friendship, if it is to be
life-giving, has to change along with times and circumstances.
Just as individuals grow, so do their friendships. By this I do
not mean the mere recycling of friends that may occur as we
move up the ladder of success and acquire what we may consider to be more "appropriate" friends. Friends who simply fit

in well with a certain lifestyle we have chosen are probably not real friends.

True friendship is tried over time. As friends continue to be open and available to one another, these bonds continue to grow; when our friends disappoint us and we them, when we are not there for each other or drop out of one another's lives, friendships wither. Sometimes these friendships can be restored, but they usually just drop by the wayside.

Friendship is also tested by circumstances. For example, our lifestyles may change completely years after the friendship was first initiated. Sometimes we entirely reject the lifestyle of our early years, and drop friends who were associated with it. If the friendship was solid enough in the first place it can survive the test of circumstances, or be revived at a later time. However, there has to be some glue, something *there* to make it worth reviving. We all have had friendships that have fizzled out into nothing, like the roaring bonfire that warms the campfire then turns to mellow coals, to a faint glow, then to ash, then nothing. Somehow there just was not enough fire, or not enough stoking, to hold the relationship together.

Our fast-paced world necessitates making new friends again and again as we move around, change jobs, move on. At every stage of our lives we gain friends. Some friends we have had from our childhood, some from high school and college. We make friends at work and in the neighborhood, through committees and the political life of our communities. We make our partner's friends our own, and sometimes we become friends to our children's friends.

Sometimes it takes a special effort to make new friends, such as learning a new language. My daughter Virginia, who lives in Uruguay, has an international group of Spanish-speaking friends. Had she not learned to speak Spanish these friendships would probably be impossible. Her children are even more fortunate: since they have absorbed both English and Spanish in equal measure, they move unconsciously between the two languages. When we moved to Paris, we were determined to have a thoroughly French experience, living far away from other Americans, but we knew that this would take special effort. So I went to a City of Paris language school two nights a week for four years, where I not only learned the language but got close to a whole group of people whom I would never otherwise encounter. My fellow students were Peruvian, Ecuadorian, Japanese, Indian, Lithuanian, Chinese, Russian, Romanian. They hailed from the former Yugoslavia and the former Soviet republics. They were Sri Lankan, Turkish, Vietnamese, Egyptian, all recent arrivals to Paris and planning to stay there for the rest of their lives. They worked at Disneyland, in factories and sweatshops. They were dishwashers, truck drivers, laborers, and maids. Nestor was a street singer with an Andean band that played in the subway stations. Samia and her husband owned a restaurant; Kenzo worked in a sushi bar; Nakita had been a doctor in Russia but in Paris he drove a taxi. We got to know each other very well by going to a café after class and having parties at holidays and at the end of every term, the tables heavy with dishes from our respective countries. And we learned French quickly because we had to—it was our only common language as we laughed our way through many mangled French pronunciations.

My efforts were magnificently rewarded, not only by the friends I made in class but especially through the friendships I made in my *quartier* where neighbors meet at the markets and in the streets, at the bakery, the cafés, and mailboxes. One day I met Madame Pélissier in the lobby of our small apartment building. She had barely spoken to me for the two years we had lived there but on this occasion she remarked, "Madame Rowthorn, I think you need a little help with your accent! Your husband speaks well enough so he does not need my help. You do!" Since this lady—a formal, stiff, very correct woman—had always seemed so aloof, I was surprised by her offer and a little nervous. Apprehensively, I arrived at her door at the appointed time and she ushered me into a small room which she had set up as a little school with dictionaries, paper and pencils, and two books, one for her and one for me, opened to a passage from Victor Hugo. Without ado she said, "Now you sit down and read a page or two, and then I will read it as it should be read!" This was not a promising beginning but I got through, and Wednesday after Wednesday it was the same. I read my way through Proust, Maritain, Flaubert, and Baudelaire, corrected constantly by Madame. And I wrote essays. We got to know each other through casual conversation, with all my errors meticulously corrected. When I had to miss a session, Madame told me to write her a letter of explanation, which she corrected with a red pen.

Throughout our time together we became close friends despite the age difference between us. The Pélissiers often invited us to dinner, and we them. We would return to Paris after a period away and M. Pélissier always invited us for a "whiskey"—which he pronounced *whee-skey*—while he shared the news we had missed while we were gone. He had been a *sur-prefet*—like a governor—of several departments (states) in France, director of agriculture in Algeria, and head of the French railroad when high-speed trains were introduced. Their friends, also our neighbors, held similar posts. An evening with them took us to the heart of recent French history and culture, and their accents were clear and lovely. We could not have had better teachers or friends.

One day at home in Paris after being away two months, I glanced from our kitchen window at M. Pélissier as he was leaving the building. He appeared a little more hunched over than usual and walked with a slightly slower step. I got the feeling that something was not just right with him—we had been back for several days and he had not invited us for the customary "whiskey." A few hours later I met Madame Bertolet at the mailboxes, and assuming I knew, she said, "Isn't it sad about Mme Pélissier dying so suddenly." I was shocked and went straight to M. Pélissier's door. Immediately upon seeing me, he hugged me for a long time and just cried and cried. All his pain poured out as if a dam had burst. From that day until we finally left Paris for good I would bring him casseroles and quiches, and he would come to us for dinner. I dreaded the day I had to tell him we were definitively returning home; almost every day after I broke the news, he asked how much more time we had left. It was as if he was keeping a countdown. Our final farewell was painful, and I still miss both M. and Mme Pélissier to this day. Had I not struggled with learning French and had Mme Pélissier not been so willing to help, I never would have encountered such special friends.

Old friends who have moved with us through life's journey are in a special category, but we all have what I would call place or activity-specific friends. We have work friends, sports friends, book club friends, political friends, hometown friends, coffee friends. In Paris I would often have my breakfast at a café adjoining an open air market. I always sat with Nanette, a ninety-two-year-old lady who was there every market day just like me. Nanette was elegant, stylish, and vivacious; she has lived all her life in the same apartment around the corner. She has lived through two world wars as well as the deaths of her husband and all her siblings. But she is a happy, canny, funny lady, very warm and always interested in my life. After I had been away for a few weeks she would be visibly relieved when I returned, and she would want to know everything that had happened since we were last together. Over time Nanette met most of my family. She gave them warm welcomes and a place at the table, and long after they had left she would unfailingly inquire about their welfare. After breakfast we would go our separate ways—Nanette had her favorite stalls and I had mine—and we would bid each other *au revoir* until the next market day.

■   ■   ■

Friendship takes many forms. Its quality runs along a continuum from casual friendships, like that of neighbors, to the deep, longstanding friendships we deliberately nourish and cultivate. Friendships may be limited to a certain place, like M. and Mme Pélissier and Nanette, or even take place in cyberspace. Friends are as essential as bread and water, as

refreshing as a cool shower on a blistering summer's day. They
are a way of measuring the richness of our lives. Through our
friends we come close to the heart of God as we nurture each
other through life's pathways of living and loving. As the Sufi
poet Rumi writes:

> To watch and listen to those two
> is to understand how, as it's written,
> sometimes when two beings come together,
> Christ becomes visible.[31]

11

Forgiveness

Reconciliation is a springtime of the heart. Yes, to become reconciled without delay leads to the amazing discovery that our own hearts are changed by it.

—Brother Roger Schutz of Taizé,
No Greater Love: Sources of Taizé

The Lewis sisters, Carrie and Elizabeth, were my next-door neighbors when I was a child. These lean, wizened, white-haired ladies who always wore exactly the same dark clothes and thick-heeled lace-up shoes had gone on living in the same house they had been born in long after their parents had passed on and their siblings moved away. It was an old-fashioned house, heated by a coal stove in the parlor and a large iron range in the kitchen, and it had a stark, lifeless feel with its dark walls and sepia pictures; only the luxuriant garden outside gave it any sense of life. We never heard any laughter coming through the open windows in summer, or music, or even cheerful conversation. There were no dogs or cats in the front yard, and no one except my mother and I ever seemed to visit the house. My mother gave the Lewis sisters presents at Christmas, and it is my guess that these were the only gifts they received. Elizabeth worked long hours at the town hospital and was away most of the time, while Carrie was the stay-at-home sister, living off her garden and supporting herself by making sumptuous chocolate-covered peppermint patties to sell at Mrs. Toff's paper and tobacco store down by the railroad station. She also sold her confections to Stowaway Sweets, a candy store made famous by Eleanor Roosevelt, who regularly ordered Carrie's candy to be sent to the White House for use on state occasions. From time to time she would give me and my brothers her candies, and sometimes she invited me in to watch her make them.

Carrie and Elizabeth—to us, of course, they were the Misses Lewis, for no child would have dreamed of calling them by their first names—were also well-known in the town for another reason. They disliked each other intensely. Neighbors reported seeing Elizabeth walking down the street toward Carrie and Carrie deliberately crossing to the other side so as not to pass directly by her sister. And vice versa. When one of the sisters went in the front door, the other left the house by the back door. It was said that when the women were teenagers they had had a bitter quarrel, and had not spoken a word to each other since.

Naively, I thought a candy-maker would be a happy person because her craft brought delight to so many, but Carrie was not; she was kind to me on occasion, but never happy. Even as a child I noticed that the lines thickly etched on her pale, translucent face were hard lines. Her jaw was tightly set and she gave the general appearance of brittleness. Although she never smiled, there was sometimes a touch of wistful warmth in her eyes, and I could see in them just a slight glimmer of life reaching out beyond her years of bitterness and resentment.

The Lewis sisters provided my first and most memorable example of what an inability to forgive looks like, and how it can diminish and even maim a life. Insult upon insult, hurt upon hurt, grudge upon grudge, year upon year, unforgiven and unresolved, leads to a half-life existence, colorless and drab, just like the lives of the Lewis sisters. Over time people *become* their negativities. Certainly no one intends to let an unforgiving life take hold of them, but unfortunately, as in the words of the *Dhammapada,* "We become what we think."

■ ■ ■

Children quickly learn that childhood is often a war of survival among the prettiest, the most handsome, the most athletic, the most popular, the best dressed, the most daring, the most trendy. These distinctions create barriers—you are either in or out of the group, and when you do not make it to the inside, your envy and resentment can build. Or perhaps one child is favored in the family. He is perceived by the parents as weaker and in need of protection, or she is more talented than the others or gets better grades in school, or perhaps is more compliant. Whatever the cause, resentments can build among the other children in the family. In the same way, naturally gifted students in high school can be the recipients of all kinds of grief from their less talented peers. They are taunted and jeered at and made to look and feel ridiculous; they have tricks played on them and their lockers are vandalized. Resentment flourishes in such fertile ground and begins to take over the character.

Later on in life, people are cheated out of the jobs they deserve or the political elections they should have won. They are cheated upon by their spouses and partners, dropped by their husbands when the "for better or for worse" becomes the worst. Or they are dropped by their friends because they do not belong to the ascendant social group, or are passed over for promotion, or are cheated out of their share in their parents' wills.

There are all kinds of good reasons for disguising the hurt we feel with resentment, and holding at a distance those who have excluded or wronged us. There are plausible reasons to keep on bearing the grudge, to bask in feelings of righteous indignation, especially when the individual or group has not taken any steps to ask for forgiveness—or are unaware of how they have offended in the first place.

But what does it cost us to forgive those who have injured us? Our pride? Or, more fundamentally, the whole structure upon which we have built our lives? What does it cost us to say, "I was wrong," or, "I am sorry"? Think of the righteous indignation of the apostle Peter, who comes to Jesus in exasperation with one of his brothers and asks, "My Lord, if my brother keeps on sinning against me, how many times do I have to forgive him? Seven times?" Imagine his reaction when Jesus answers him, "No, you must forgive your brother seventy times seven."

No one ever said that forgiving was easy. Its difficulty is borne out by the many people, ourselves included, who nurse a hurt and carry a grudge rather than forgive it and drop it. Does the degree to which one is hurt influence one's readiness to forgive? It is easy to apologize for walking on a newly seeded lawn or for a spilled drink or a small misunderstanding. It is more difficult to forgive the doctor who amputates the wrong leg or the estranged husband who strikes his children in a drunken rage. On the public stage, does one forgive even the most heinous and detestable criminals of all time? Are Jews whose families were tortured in concentration camps supposed to forgive the Nazis? As I write these pages today, word has just reached me that Brother Roger, the beloved founder and leader of the Taizé community in France, has been brutally murdered during the evening prayer service in the presence of several thousand young people. Are we to forgive the deranged woman who stabbed him?

■   ■   ■

What is the place of anger? Catherine, the central character in Sue Miller's novel *The World Below*, thinks back on her two broken marriages and wonders whether she could have swallowed her hurts and stayed with her partners. "Would the price have been the pushing under of whatever enraged or disappointed each of us in the other? . . . Or was that forgiveness at all, if anger still lived underneath the peace?"[32] Can we really forgive when we are still angry? Does anger have to subside before forgiveness becomes possible? What is the place of remembering? In the small disagreements children have with one another, their parents are likely to tell them to "forgive and forget." But if it is a life-size adult offense, can we realistically forgive and forget?

All these are salient questions, and none are easily answered. On the other hand, a few things can be said about forgiveness that would apply whether it is a nation or a people or an individual who does the forgiving. Forgiving our deepest hurts may take time because such an act requires a real turning around, even a conversion, and this may not happen overnight. It may take time to replace resentment with acceptance, pride with humility, negative feelings with positive ones. We can remember and still forgive; in fact the collective memory of wrongful and even evil acts may be some insurance against their recurrence. Behind Notre Dame Cathedral in Paris there is a small but arresting memorial to the French victims of Nazi concentration camps. Two hundred thousand small lights, representing each person who died, gleam beyond the engraving over the arch at the entrance, which says, "Forgive, Do Not Forget."

Michael and Kathy were walking to church one bright summer evening with their children, Jonathan and Rachael, when a car sideswiped them, killing Rachael instantly and leaving Kathy paralyzed from the waist down. When Bonnie's headache was discovered to be caused by a brain tumor, the surgeon assured her that he could remove it—but he cut a nerve in the process, leaving half her beautiful face frozen. Nelson Mandela took a stand against the system of apartheid in South Africa and spent twenty-eight years behind bars. Two women, one Catholic and the other Protestant, lost family members and friends in the violence of Northern Ireland. It took time, but all of these people learned to forgive—Michael and Kathy, the driver who sideswiped their family; Bonnie, the surgeon whose knife slipped; Mandela, the white state authorities whose trumped-up charges held him captive; the women of Londonderry, the killers of their loved ones. However heinous the deed, however much the anger, no matter whether the offending person or group does anything to deserve forgiveness, and however long it takes—deep, authentic forgiveness must occur. As Brother Roger of Taizé told us, "Reconciliation is the springtime of the heart. Yes, to become reconciled without delay leads to the amazing discovery that our own hearts are changed by it."

▪ ▪ ▪

While my first experience of seeing what happens when we do not forgive came through the bitter lives of the Lewis sisters, my most powerful experience of forgiveness came many years later at a Lambeth Conference, the meeting of Anglican bishops and their spouses from around the world held in Canterbury, England. The community of Anglican bishops comes together every ten years for fellowship, to get to know and appreciate what is going on in each other's region of the world, and to discuss the issues that confront the church as a whole. A major part of this meeting consists of Bible study every morning, all morning, the bishops meeting in their own groups and the spouses in theirs. When I was asked to lead one of the two French-speaking groups, I quickly accepted. My group would include women from the some of the hardest, most challenging places on the planet, such as Burundi, Rwanda, and the Congo, and I would be exposed to a world vastly different from my own. I would be able to hear their own stories in their own words, not filtered through a translator. I also felt that, as a native English-speaker struggling with French, my second language, I would perhaps come to understand more fully the efforts of immigrants the world over who are forced to make themselves understood in the languages of others.

I was the only non-African member of the group. All eleven women had lived in extreme poverty, and everyone from Rwanda, the Congo, or Burundi had seen friends and family members killed in the genocide. They had personally witnessed pillages, rape, massacres of all kinds, babies butchered out of their mothers' stomachs, and other atrocities. In addition to having five or six children of their own, they were also taking into their homes nieces and nephews, neighborhood youngsters; children whose parents had been murdered. Some were also sheltering widows. The Congo should be one of the richest countries in the world, with fertile soil, vast mineral wealth, and a river whose force could provide enough electricity for the entire African continent, yet its forty-four million people are among the poorest on earth. They endured thirty-two years of ethnic hatred, brutality, killings, chaos, and misery under the harsh rule of Joseph Mobutu; the dictator is now dead, but by the summer of Lambeth Conference ethnic struggles had begun to erupt anew.

The themes of St. Paul's second letter to the Corinthians, which we read and studied together in our morning Bible study, spoke with great clarity to us all. Forgiveness, mutual openness to God, living justly, giving generously, finding hope and joy in serving Christ—these biblical values have been tested again and again in the lives of our group members. And the news from overseas reminded us poignantly of the immediacy of their suffering. One morning Pascaline came in with the news that one hundred twenty-nine people had been killed in her home diocese in the Congo. A week later Josephine gave us the first reports of the American embassy bombing in Nairobi. We heard this news against the background of Paul's words about the early Christians, "We are afflicted in every way, but not crushed; perplexed, but not driven to despair; persecuted, but not forsaken; struck down, but not destroyed" (2 Corinthians 4:8–9).

I had expected to learn about suffering and tragedy from these women, but I had not expected to be bowled over by their profound, unshakable faith. They put a human face on the tremendous sufferings of the African continent. The grim statistics of Africa now represent friends and family of people

I have come to know and to care about very much. These brave women are the embodiment of both the crucifixion and the resurrection of Jesus, and most of all, they are living examples to me of what forgiveness means. Their deep joy and love were infectious.

Grace and her husband are from two opposing ethnic groups, Tutsi and Hutu, in Rwanda. His brothers, who disapproved of his marriage, took out their revenge by killing all of Grace's Tutsi relatives. Following their vicious murder, Grace said, she cried for weeks; her tears flowed like a river without end. She lay awake in bed in the still of the night, vigilant and watchful, wondering when they would come after her. The murdering brothers are now in prison, but while they were at large, Grace's life was a living hell.

Now, Grace told me, she prays for her brothers-in-law every day, visits them in prison, and brings them food. When I asked her how she could possibly do this, she shrugged and with a gentle smile simply told me that she believes Jesus' words are true—that we should love our enemies and pray for those who persecute us. We cannot repay wrong with wrong, she said, but must do everything possible to live in peace with everyone. When I asked her if she had genuinely forgiven her brothers-in-law, she again smiled and told me she had.

Now, years later, Grace is able to see the men as human beings and she says she feels real sympathy for them. She is sorry that for such an impulsive and rash act they have to spend the rest of their days in jail. She feels for them. There is sadness in Grace's large, beautiful eyes and it is evident that the pain is still there, but I could detect neither bitterness nor resentment. When she is not thinking about the tragedy, Grace is cheerful and even joyful. She is living gracefully and at peace with herself. To me Grace will forever remain an arresting example of the great lengths to which a human being can go to forgive.

Forgiving opens up the heart. It is the gift already in your hands. Open it and let it flow.

12

Your Daily Life is Your Temple

Your daily life is your religion and your temple.
—Kahlil Gibran, *The Prophet*

This morning is just like every other at Herman's Diner in Colchester, Connecticut. With a wide smile, Jane Bittman, the owner, is greeting late arrivals for breakfast just as she has done for the past twenty-seven years. She knows exactly how the regulars like their coffee and whether they want their eggs over easy or scrambled. While she and Diane pour coffee and tend the grill they are talking to everyone and asking how they are, checking on their families. Today is Friday, so the lunch specials are baked stuffed flounder with a choice of a baked potato or potato salad, along with a garden salad on the side; and barbecued baby back ribs, baked beans, and a salad.

Between cooking my bacon, egg, and cheese on an English muffin and turning the hash browns, Jane checks in the oven below to see how the flounder is doing. Phyllis is sitting at the end of the counter in front of an enormous bowl of potatoes she has just peeled. Jane introduces me: "She's a customer who volunteers four to five mornings a week to help us out." Phyllis has recently moved into a retirement center and has some spare time: "This is the greatest thing I do. It's what gets me up in the morning and gets me out. I always leave the diner happy, and any troubles I thought I had are forgotten." Next to her, Jennie pipes up: "When Phyllis is sick I come in and help get lunch ready." When regular customers miss coming in for several days, Jane will either phone them or send over some food. Everyone sitting at the counter says it is the family feeling that keeps them coming in, day after day. As I pay my bill, Jane sends her best wishes to my husband and son, and as I drive away I marvel at the profound difference Jane and her community of volunteers and guests make to the life of one small corner of Connecticut.

This book began with a simple definition of a spirituality of everyday life in today's world, which is simply everything we all do all day long to build up the commonwealth of God. It is the gift already in our hands. While my examples of people who live a spirituality of everyday life come from around the world, I end the book with Jane. She illustrates to me an authentic spirituality of someone who has lived intensely at home close to her roots. Jane opens the gift every morning at her diner.

■   ■   ■

As I drive the eight miles home I pass Walt's Country Motors, where Walt and his son Bill are busy replacing mufflers and changing oil, doing tune-ups and lubes. I stop by Swiders' Farm where the Swider family sells delicious fresh vegetables and succulent blueberries, peaches, and plums, and today, as always, Mrs. Swider tucks an extra ear of corn into my shopping bag. I continue past the Maple Shade where Dave sells gas, propane, and a few groceries, runs a trash collection service and post office, and plows driveways in the winter. Next door is the Salem Volunteer Fire Company, then the Town Hall and the library. I pass the Salem School and notice that the parking lot is full and remember that school starts next week and the teachers are there preparing their classrooms and doing in-service training. As I pass the artist Annie Pugsley's house, I wonder what she's painting now and what her discerning eye is seeing and capturing on her canvas. Driving into Salem Four Corners, I pass the video store, the bank, package store, ice cream bar, hair dresser, pizza parlor, motorcycle show room, doctor's and dentist's offices, and the Coffee Connection—all are open and doing business. They form the web that keeps our town connected, healthy, nourished, cared for, educated, and passionately engaged in the world around us. Without them our town could not flourish. Each institution, craft, and service, both public and private, provides something essential to our life. They are all gifts which, once opened, reveal the presence of God in our lives. They are everywhere and they are deep within—these are the temples of our daily lives.

Jim Cunningham crafts an oak floor and a new roof and he builds not only a house but a life, as does Ed Todd, the Rhode Island fisherman who feels the majesty of God as his trawler sails under the rainbow out at sea. Mechanics, factory workers, bankers, lawyers, greeters at department stores, waitresses, cashiers, bartenders, construction workers, lawyers, teachers, and long-distance truck drivers build up the fabric of the world. Children are also windows into the temples of our daily lives. Sometimes they take us to suffering corners of the world, such as Darfur in the Sudan, where twelve-year-old Micah Allen-Doucot went with his father. Byron Rushing, Lallie Lloyd, and Judith Lockhart-Radtke show us what one person can do to make a difference in the political and economic lives of communities, both at home and far away. Opening their gifts of passion for a better and more just world, they show us how we all can use whatever we have to promote justice, goodness, and liberation.

Perhaps my most enduring example of a practicing spirituality of everyday life is an old woman called Beatrice Dodge, who had lived all her life on the small islands off the Maine coast and in the tiny communities near Ellsworth. When we met her she was living much as she had for the past seventy-five years, on the edge of the Union River Bay in a hamlet known as Bayside. As a child she went with her grandfather by horse and wagon to Bangor to sell their clams and lobsters, helped her mother tend the family's sheep, dyeing and spinning the wool. When we knew her, she went to the supermarket about once every two weeks, whenever she could get a ride, but other than that she carried on the daily affairs of her life just as she always had, centered on her house and garden and the shore. She planted and tended the garden in the summer; she canned vegetables for the winter. She gathered mussels, crabs, wild blueberries, and edible ferns from the shore. She cleaned and dried fish caught from the bay. One of her pastimes in the winter was making extraordinarily beautiful hooked rugs. She crafted them out of grain sacks and cotton remnants she got from the textile mill a few miles away in Bangor. They were the illuminated manuscripts of Granny's life, with scenes taken from her surroundings—the barn and the house, fishing boats, deer, seagulls, apple trees, boulders, and pine trees that lined the shore across the street.

Hers was a world of natural plenty and extravagant beauty, but with few material possessions. When the first of the Dodge children was born, George Dodge ended his tenure on an outer island where he had been a lighthouse keeper and he never again had a job with regular hours, pay, and benefits, but both George and Beatrice made enough money to provide for their family. They knew all the signs of nature that bore intimately on the welfare and sometimes even the survival of the family. George read the currents and the seasons. He knew the varieties of fish, when they were running and where they could best be caught. He had a few well-placed lobster traps in the bay that rarely came up empty; he kept the family well supplied and sold the extra to his neighbors and the summer people. Theirs was also a world where neighbors helped each other with large tasks such as hauling logs and building barns, and while each family prided itself on its independence, neighbors were there for each other in times of need. While life was far from easy and there could be droughts, shortages, and red tides poisoning the fish, the Dodges' life was one of passionate engagement with all its rhythms.

Although I might have liked to think of Granny Dodge as a churchgoer, she was not. Apart from telling us about the day she was baptized off the rocky shore at Seawall, she had little to say about religion of any kind. While she was poetic and artistic, she was not given to reflection. She lived entirely in the present, and never bored us with suggesting that things were better at some earlier time. Although she had endured many losses, she was not bowed down by them or by any of the regrets in her life. She was fully alive, fully awake, as a Buddhist might say. Just like Jane Bittman, Granny Dodge reveals to me what it is like to be passionately engaged in the everyday, the temple of her daily life.

■ ■ ■

Whether we travel the skyways of the world or stay at home, or anything in between, an authentic spirituality where we seek and meet God every moment of our lives is there for each one of us. It is a gift already in our hands, beckoning us to unwrap and to behold.

Gregory F. Augustine Pierce, a Roman Catholic who has devoted his life to helping people see their daily lives as sacred, recounts the story from Buddhist tradition of the woman who finally became enlightened. When she was asked what difference being enlightened made to her, she said, "Before I was enlightened, I chopped wood and I hauled water. After I was enlightened, I chopped wood and I hauled water."[33] Like her, when we come into the awareness that our daily life is our temple, the outward aspects of our lives may not change at all: we will still be chopping wood. We will be living where we always did, doing our same jobs, taking care of our children, making our money talk, participating in the public life of our communities, enjoying the arts, loving our friends, and forgiving one another. What changes is our awareness that our daily life is our religion and our temple, that everything true and good and sacred is right here, right now.

Endnotes

1. Dorothee Soelle, *The Silent Cry* (Minneapolis: Fortress Press, 2001), 298.

2. Richard Bernstein, *Ultimate Journey: Retracing the Path of an Ancient Buddhist Monk Who Crossed Asia in Search of Enlightenment* (New York: Random House/Vintage Books, 2002), 32–33.

3. Kurama Temple, "Prayer of Love, Light and Power," from *Prayer for the Happiness to the Sonten of Kuramayama* (Kyoto, Japan: Kurama Temple, no date). Used by permission of Kurama Temple.

4. *Dhammapada,* chp. 1, v. 1 and 2 *passim*. In *The Dhammapada,* trans. Eknath Eswaran (Tomalas, Calif.: Nilgari Press, 1985), 78.

5. Quoted in an interview with Gustav Niebuhr, "Acknowledging That God is Not Limited to Christians," *The New York Times* (June, 2003).

6. Pope John Paul II, *On Human Work: Laborem Excercens* (Washington, D. C.: U. S. Catholic Conference, September 14, 1981), 10.

7. "Graham Reaches Workday Milestone: 250 Different Jobs Equals a Workyear," press release for March 27, 1991.

8. From a sermon preached by Archbishop Oscar Romero on January 27, 1980.

9. Dorothee Soelle, *To Work and To Love: A Theology of Creation* (Philadelphia: Fortress Press, 1984), 103, 112.

10. Sam Keen, *Apology for Wonder* (New York: Harper and Row Publishers, 1969), 43–44.

11. Soelle, *To Work and To Love,* 47.

12. Children of Yugoslavia, in *Children's State of the Planet Handbook* (Hilversum, the Netherlands: Peace Child International, 2002), 6.

13. Interview with Robert Coles in the video *Listening to Children: A Moral Journey with Robert Coles* (Social Media Productions and the Center for Documentary Studies at Duke University, 1995).

14. "Helping a Slowly Moving Good Cause," *The Hartford Catholic Worker* (Easter 2005), 3–4 *passim*.

15. Quoted in Anthony L. Geist and Peter N. Carroll, *Children's Art in Wartime: They Still Draw Pictures: Children's Art from the Spanish Civil War to Kosovo* (Urbana and Chicago: University of Illinois Press, 2002), 9.

16. Quoted in Raymond Rousset, *The Ways of Light: Van Gogh in the Land of Arles* (Monaco: Société Ajax, 1994), 19.

17. Rousset, *Ways of Light,* 19.

18. Quoted in Andre Verdet, *Chagall's World: Reflections from the Mediterranean* (Garden City, N. Y.: Doubleday and Company, Inc., 1984), 57.

19. Quoted in Cliff Edwards, *Van Gogh and God* (Chicago: Loyola University Press, 1989), 160.

20. Quoted in John Dillenberger and Jane Dillenberger, *On Art and Architecture* (New York: Crossroad, 1987), 15–16.

21. Frederick Franck, *The Zen of Seeing: Seeing/Drawing as Meditation* (New York: Random House/Vintage Books, 1973), x, 8.

22. Helen Caldicott, *Missile Envy: The Arms Race and Nuclear War* (Hammondsmith, Middlesex, England: Bantam Books, 1985), 367.

23. From "A Community of the Spirit," in *The Essential Rumi,* trans. Coleman Barks (San Francisco: HarperSanFrancisco, 1995), 3.

24. From "Apology" in H. L. Milne, "A New Fragment of the Apology of Aristides," *Journal of Theological Studies* 25 (1924): 217.

25. Christine D. Pohl, *Making Room: Recovering Hospitality as a Christian Tradition* (Grand Rapids: Eerdmans, 1999), 6.

26. Timothy Fry, OSB, *The Rule of St. Benedict* (Collegeville, Minn.: Liturgical Press, 1981), chp. 23, 255–256.

27. Kathleen Norris, *The Cloister Walk* (New York: Riverhead Books, 1996), 367.

28. See Sabina Alkire and Edmund Newell, eds., *What Can One Person Do?* (New York: Church Publishing, 2005).

29. Gregory F. A. Pierce, *Spirituality@Work* (Chicago: Loyola Press, 2001), 106–107.

30. From an interview with Don McClanen and Bryan Sirchio, Mill Valley, California, on October 4, 2003.

31. Rumi, "A Mouse and a Frog," in *Essential Rumi,* 79.

32. Sue Miller, *The World Below* (New York: Random House, 2001), 132.

33. Pierce, *Spirituality@Work,* 3.